WHAT
GREAT
LOOKS
LIKE

Leadership Best Practices
for General Managers

JEREMEY
DONOVAN

ISBN: 1456464477
ISBN-13: 9781456464479

Contents

Introduction

Every day, successful individual contributors are rewarded by being thrust into general management roles. As one of my mentors likes to say, "the reward for winning the hot dog eating contest is more hot dogs." Even those lucky enough to have earned a Masters in Business Administration are ill prepared for the daily challenges that await them. Newly minted leaders need a set of best practices and lessons learned to guide them to excellence.

I wrote this book with the aim of giving current and aspiring general managers a competitive edge by sharing my take on what great looks like in leadership, strategy, marketing, innovation, and professional development. The guidance is drawn from my own experience as well as from stories spanning academia, nonfiction business literature, and popular media. In particular, I have focused on applied general management skills that were not covered in my otherwise excellent education at the University of Chicago Booth School of Business.

In researching the material for this book, I read countless business best sellers. The finest of these are listed in the recommended reading section at the end. Among the books I combed through, a few were themselves compilations that digested popular literature into one or two page summaries. These summaries stimulated my interest in the underlying works, but left me wanting for more knowledge. I craved something more comprehensive than a single page and something more efficient than an entire book. My aim here is to bridge that gap. I hope the insights in this book give you a competitive edge in your professional endeavors.

PART ONE:

MANAGING
AND
LEADERSHIP

Chapter One: Leadership

It has often been said, and correctly so, that leaders are made, not born. But, to embark on a journey of becoming a leader, you first have to know what a great leader looks like. At the end of the day, people that are perceived as great leaders inspire others to accomplish more than they could do alone. Here is how to do just that.

Craft and Communicate A Shared Vision
That Is Positive, Concrete, and Forward-Looking

If the successful leadership recipe has one central ingredient, it is crafting and communicating a positive, forward-looking shared vision. To inspire, a vision must tell people what the goal is, why it matters, and how they will achieve it.

Importantly, a great vision must be easy to communicate. Vision is the voice whispering in people's ears that inspires individual initiative and empowers them to venture into uncertainty. Moreover, to be successful, your vision must be capable of being transferred virally from person to person, since you cannot be there most of the time. That can happen only if your vision is concise and concrete.

On a visceral level, human beings derive personal fulfillment by making life better for themselves and for others. In periods of adversity, a great vision should deliver a response to a personally relevant external threat. In periods of opportunity, a great vision should provide a realizable individual benefit and offer people a way to change the world.

Imagine it is April 4, 1975 and you are sitting in an Albuquerque, New Mexico coffee shop with Bill Gates and Paul Allen. Bill has just dropped out of Harvard, relocated across the country, and started a new company called Micro-Soft with fellow dropout Paul (they later removed the hyphen). The company's first product is software that interprets and executes simple programs written in the then ten year old BASIC language. Bill and Paul could have crafted a competitive vision such as 'crush Digital Equipment Corporation, Data General, and Hewlett Packard by dominating the BASIC programming language market.' Yet, they must have sensed that purely competitive visions are negative by definition. Though sustainable in the short term, negative emotions cannot - or at the very least should not - be sustained. And, what happens if you win? What's next?

Instead, according to legend, the Microsoft founders articulated the vision 'a computer on every desk and in every home, running Microsoft software.' It certainly worked for them, but it could have been better. This vision does have a concrete outcome and is forward looking, but it neither tells employees what is in it for them personally nor does it show how their collective effort will make the world a better place.

Eventually, they got it right. Microsoft's current vision is 'to help people and businesses throughout the world realize their full potential.' Whether or not you like Microsoft, you have to respect the leadership and vision of Bill Gates.

Recruit, hire, and continually train the very best people you can to become leaders themselves

For any great leader, time spent recruiting exceptional people offers the single greatest return on investment available. Even in organizations of modest size, leaders fly in a hyper-speed orbit of guide-measure-iterate, guide-measure-iterate, with limited time for execution. Hence, the people responsible for building products and delivering services are ultimately responsible for the success or failure of the organization.

At some point in your professional life, undoubtedly you have had a terrible partner, employee, peer, or supervisor. If so, you remember that experience vividly. Left unchecked, this type of person will destroy your vision and your organization. Equally important, a 'bad-egg' consumes your most precious asset – time – without any positive return. An ounce of prevention is worth a pound of cure so you need to recruit well to lead well.

Ideally, you should recruit the best people, period. However, practically, you should set your sights on recruiting the best people you can, given your circumstances. All leaders have constraints on the position they are seeking to fill: constraints on salary, location, talent pool, etc. Once you know your constraints, take as much time as you have available to ensure that you are hiring the very best person possible.

Once you have hired, you bear a weighty personal and professional responsibility to help people achieve their personal hopes and dreams through their work. If you did your job during the hiring process, the individual fully understood and fully embraced your vision. Since your employees spend more hours working for you than just about anything else they do, fulfilling the vision must be inextricably linked to their hopes and dreams. When the connection is made, daily work naturally will imbue people with direction and a sense of purpose.

Great leaders empower individuals to reach their potential with daily opportunities for growth. Though not everyone wants to climb the corporate ladder to the top, everyone does crave professional development of one form or another. Otherwise they will die of boredom in their jobs, or, less dramatically, leave your organization. Ask people what they believe their strengths are and what skills they are seeking to develop. Invest time to determine their strengths and the new skills that would make them stronger. Then, make sure that the objectives you set and the tasks you give offer daily chances to learn.

The ultimate gift of great leaders is training people to become great leaders themselves. This is not only the best form of intangible compensation, but also the most surefire way to guarantee the current and future success of your organization and the fulfillment of your vision.

Mobilize people and harness resources

As a great leader, you now have the critical ingredients for success — an inspiring vision combined with talented, highly motivated people. Left to their own devices, people will chart their own course to fulfill your shared vision. Though admirable, this approach will result in a poor use of limited resources.

Instead, you must prioritize and share a key set of objectives to amplify and accelerate success. To be successful, your goals should be realistically based on existing or planned organizational resources and capabilities. Through that lens, you can accept or reject proposed activities. The greatest leaders go one step further by satisfying multiple priorities with each activity. Additionally, stellar leaders maniacally make sure to involve the right people whose extrinsic and intrinsic motivations are aligned with achieving the strategic objective.

Great leaders keep their prioritized set of objectives front and center by creating and managing momentum. Short term wins do not happen by accident; you must painstakingly plan for them and then tirelessly promote them. When people achieve meaningful short term wins, they proudly redouble their efforts to reach the next milestone.

Earn and maintain trust

People accept only leaders they trust. Early 20th century oil entrepreneur J. Paul Getty embraced this concept long before the term managerial psychology had been coined and at a time when robber-barons were little evolved from feudal tyrants. Trust must come from the heart and trust must be proactively earned and maintained.

Getty built trust by modeling the way. Though born into the family oil business and well educated at elite universities, Getty routinely got his hands dirty joining his men on the rigs. Maniacally focused on cost control, he was known to sleep in his car and later in budget motels. Once, when an executive in his company took home some scrap but still useful wood to build a doghouse, Getty very publicly compelled the executive to pay the company back. If the man had not otherwise been an exemplary employee, Getty would have fired him to make an even better example of him.

Though great leaders possess poise, they know that credibility does not require perfection. Quite to the contrary, it is important to show people that you are human. J. Paul Getty did this by publicly acknowledging the mistakes he made along the way to success. For example, he cited his loss of conviction despite careful due diligence in an oil investment after his partners lost faith during early

1930's stock market volatility. Take careful note that Getty paired his mistakes with the important learning he gleaned in the process.

In one-on-one interactions, great leaders earn and maintain trust through two essential practices. The first is to give credit and take blame. If you never falter in this practice, your reputation will precede you as you inspire your people and attract new talent. The second is to show people that your belief in their ability exceeds their own belief in their ability. In so doing, you will assuage people's self doubts and insecurities. In following this simple practice, you will give your people the fuel they need to achieve their full potential.

Strive to become "sought after"

In addition to having trust in their leaders, people must believe that those who wish to lead them have the ability to chart the course. When investing in their own personal and professional development, strong leaders set objectives that make them "sought after" in ways that are directly relevant to the realization of their vision.

Even before J. Paul Getty had great wealth, seasoned oil field workers abandoned the relative comfort of neighboring drilling operations to join his austere operation. His sought-after ability to strike oil far outweighed the sacrifice in working conditions].

As a great leader you are building a brand. Even in the unlikely event that you could gain the widely varied expertise of a polymath, people will only be able to identify you with a very small number of attributes. Figure out the skills in which you excel that align with your vision and then invest tirelessly to improve and to share your knowledge.

Recap

Here are the concepts you can immediately apply to become a great leader:
- Craft and communicate a shared vision that is positive, concrete, and forward-looking
- Recruit, hire, and continually train the very best people you can to become leaders themselves

- Mobilize people and harness resources
- Earn and maintain trust
- Strive to become "sought after"

Chapter Two: Problem Solving

Problems are ubiquitous and arise daily. Despite that fact, parents, schools, and organizations rarely teach structured problem solving skills. Our culture then expresses surprise at divorce rates for first marriages over forty percent and at rampant corporate inefficiency that manifests itself in disappointing profits, high employee turnover, and stunning customer service breakdowns.

Management consulting firms are the one exception to the problem solving training vacuum. New associates are indoctrinated in a veritable alphabet soup of frameworks such as 7S, 5 Why's, 4P's, Five Forces, SWOT, and so on. While management consultants should master as many useful frameworks as possible, managers should pick the one they find most valuable and stick to it. Though no single approach can solve every type of problem, you should strive to consistently use a single system that is both simple to apply and that works in most situations.

This chapter delivers a framework that meets both criteria. Those practiced in problem solving techniques will recognize this as a variant on the situation-complication-resolution framework with a few twists thrown in.

Define the problem and make sure it is worth solving

Most problem-solving frameworks leave off the single most important first step — understanding the problem and making sure it is worth solving. Even modest sized organizations have hundreds if not thousands of problems. There are inefficiencies in production, service delivery, personnel, and on and on.

Economics courses routinely teach the importance of accounting for opportunity costs of capital. There are of course tremendous opportunity costs of time and energy that lurk beneath every decision to resolve a particular problem. You must spend enough time thinking about the range of problems that need solving and target the low hanging fruit possessing the greatest return on investment. As you do this, never lose sight of business and societal ethics; more directly, immediately prioritize problems that represent threats to environmental health and safety.

To rank problems – high, medium, low will do – you must visualize, at least at a conceptual level, what the outcomes look like. The litmus test of whether or not a problem is worth solving is whether or not the solution meets primary strategic objectives. January 28th, 1986 confronted President Ronald Reagan with a particularly stark example of this, when space shuttle Challenger and its seven-member crew perished in a nationally televised fireball seventy-three seconds after launch. In the aftermath, beyond the obvious moral imperative to figure out what happened, the United States needed to get the space shuttle program back on track in the interest of national defense. At the time, the country was deeply embroiled in the Cold War and space supremacy signaled to the Soviet Union that United States warheads posed an unambiguous nuclear deterrent. Moreover, in order to maintain faith in their government, American citizens needed to know that they would not be annihilated by their own arsenal. For President Reagan, the outcome of getting the space shuttle program back on track clearly met the primary strategic objectives of maintaining national defense and faith in government.

Though less dramatic, businesses must prioritize problem solving as well. Suppose you work for a firm with high fixed costs and low variable costs and whose customers make repeat purchases at some reasonable frequency. Three primary strategic objectives for you are likely customer acquisition, customer retention, and sales effectiveness. All three of these drive revenue growth. By contrast, operational efficiencies that drive cost control are secondary objectives rarely worth prioritizing unless you compete in a totally commoditized space.

Very often, people will present you with a collection of symptoms or with a request for you to embark on a labor intensive solution such as a complex analytical task. Slow them down and ask two questions. First, ask 'What is the problem you are trying to solve?' Second, ask them and yourself 'Is this problem worth solving?'. The former question allows you to understand the outcome, to diagnose their approach, and to think of creative out-of-the-box alternatives. If you are problem solving with others, you need to agree on the outcome. The latter question tells you whether or not you should bother in the first place.

Form an initial hypothesis

From your earliest days, you were probably told to wait until you had sufficient facts before forming an opinion or making a judgment. We take as undeniable truth expressions such as "Don't judge a book by its cover" or "Avoid making decisions based on first impressions." Though great advice when browsing for a book or a potential mate, this advice is flat out wrong during the initial phases of problem solving.

When confronted with a problem to solve, immediately form a hypothesis. Remember that a hypothesis is merely a proposed explanation that must be rigorously tested. A good problem solver will search for facts, all the while updating their hypothesis. Great problem solvers not only seek information that confirms their hypothesis but also mercilessly hunt for disconfirming information.

In statistics, a hypothesis can never be accepted. Rather, your only options are to either reject or fail-to-reject the hypothesis. Statistics loves uncertainty and this treatment of testing your hypotheses leaves an air of mystery. When you think about it, decisions in your personal or professional life are pretty much that way too. You can never know with absolute certainty that you are making the right or best decision; you do the best you can with the information you have at the time.

Merely failing to reject something feels pretty unimpressive. It is a lot more definitive to outright reject something. Hence, statisticians always construct their hypotheses (known as the null hypotheses) to test the opposite of what they think is true. By trying to prove the opposite of what you believe, you are forcing yourself to take the high road of seeking disconfirming information.

An example will clarify. Let's say you believe that taller people make more money (as psychologists Timothy Judge and Daniel Cable theorized in a 2004 study). For starters, you might have some decent data that taller people make more money. The best approach is to play devil's advocate and posit reasons why taller people might actually make equal or less money. To do that, you should get as much data as you can on people, data that includes not only wage and height information, but also physical and socioeconomic descriptors. Next, remove the influence of gender, weight, age, industry of employment, and so on. Keep searching for material (or information) that would explain why taller people earn more money than their diminutive friends other than height itself. In the end, if you cannot find anything, then you can sleep pretty well at night with your hypothesis that taller people are better remunerated. (For the record, according to Judge and Cable's study, every inch of height adds $789 per year.)

Understand the current situation

Before delving into problems and brainstorming solutions, you first need to understand how you got here and what the current state of the world is. Though vital even when you problem solve alone, this is downright critical when you are problem solving with others, since they need unbiased facts and context to be able to lend their full mental muscle.

With that in mind, let's revisit the Challenger disaster. Formed on February 3, 1986, the Rogers Commission started laying out the facts. What was the timeline in the hours, minutes, and seconds leading up to the explosion? What was the temperature on the launch pad? What processes and procedures were followed in the mission control room? Who manufactured the shuttle's various components and to what specifications? Like the Commissions' fact list, yours needs to be neither too elementary nor too comprehensive. Yet, while not being exhaustive, ideally the list of facts should give a nearly complete context to the problem you are solving and start to uncover the levers that might be used to fix it.

In laying out the specifics, you want to consider structural information as well as behavioral information. Structural information includes physical and descriptive attributes such as time, temperature, geography, and industry. Behavioral information captures the human element including attitudes, actual processes, and the like. Between the two, behavioral information requires more heavy lifting to obtain. The effort will be well rewarded, however, because in most circumstances, it is the behavioral information that holds the key to solving the problem.

The fastest and most effective way to capture behavioral information is through interviewing. Take any population, say flight safety engineers, and identify your best performing employees and your worst. In doing so, you must select candidates by applying objective measures such as the number of missed safety violations, not subjective measures such as managers' opinions. Now, interview both groups and ascertain what the top performers do differently than the bottom. In the case of the Challenger investigation, the Rogers Commission interviewed more than 160 individuals. In most business settings, interviewing ten to twenty people is sufficient.

Uncover the complications

Once you have articulated the current situation, you must now find specific complications and occasionally hidden opportunities. In your first pass, you should enumerate the distinct, comprehensive set of top level complications. Resist the urge to deep dive on individual issues. In subsequent passes, drill down one level deeper at a time.

The more information you have, the surer you will be that you have identified the true root of the problem. First, you need to examine structural data. As the Challenger disaster played out in an endless loop on television, hot exhaust gases could be seen escaping from the rubber o-rings that were supposed to seal the joints on the shuttle's solid rocket boosters. Looking back at past shuttle launches, Roger Boisjoly — an engineer working for solid rocket booster manufacturer Morton Thiokol —found that potentially catastrophic exhaust gas leaks occurred around o-rings every time the temperature fell below freezing. With launch day temperatures hovering around eighteen degrees Fahrenheit, the space shuttle was doomed before takeoff. The striking exclamation point was made on this structural complication on February 11, 1986 when Nobel Laureate Richard Feynman famously dunked an o-ring in a glass of ice water during a Rogers Commission hearing. When he pulled the rubber ring from the water, the ring had lost its resiliency.

Feynman not only dramatized the o-ring structural complication but also relentlessly pursued behavioral complications to the apparent dismay of commission chairman William Rogers, who reportedly characterized Feynman as "becoming a real pain." As it turned out, Roger Boisjoly warned both his employer and

NASA about the poor low-temperature performance of the o-rings as early as six months before the tragedy.

Select a resolution that can be executed

In the final stage of problem solving, you should articulate the range of possible resolutions and identify the best one as the recommended option. Each resolution should be clearly described and should include potential benefits and risks. An excellent best practice is to characterize benefits as either primary or secondary in order to maintain focus on what truly matters. In addition, acknowledging risks as known and acceptable prevents the unknown from paralyzing the decision making process. If behavioral complications are at the root of the problem, as they often are, you are likely going to get the most mileage teaching the best practices of your best performers to the rest of your organization.

In business settings, a great resolution has two necessary preconditions. First, the solution must leverage existing capabilities in the form of both resources and knowledge. An elegant solution that cannot be executed is worthless. Second, the solution must carry strong executive commitment or the organization will never embrace the necessary change.

The Rogers Commission could have recommended doing nothing (an oft underconsidered option though rightly ruled out in this case), discontinuing the existing space shuttle program, or making structural and behavioral modifications to the program; They chose the last, suggesting nine sweeping modifications that spanned redesigning the solid rocket booster joints and seals, overhauling the shuttle management structure, improving safety controls, and decreasing the shuttle launch rate.

To its credit, the Rogers Commission achieved the final component of a great resolution. Specifically, its members embraced the concept of test, then measure, then iterate. In their directive to redesign the solid rocket booster joints and seals, they required that certification include "Tests which duplicate the actual launch configuration as closely as possible." As for measurement, the final report called for NASA to "perform periodic structural inspections when scheduled and not permit them to be waived." The test-measure-iterate sequence is as essential in business as it is in space travel.

Recap

Your objective as a great problem solver is to become a trusted thought partner. Consider the difference between an impressive associate and a great partner. Talented associates can encounter any situation and draw compelling insights. They can expertly and concisely extract the so-what. In contrast, exceptional partners do two things. First, they maintain the hypothesis defining the full vision for the final solution. As they receive new confirming and disconfirming information, they update the hypothesis. Second, and equally important, they are expert in communicating the vision every step of the way.

Here are the concepts you can immediately apply to be a great problem solver:
- Define the problem and make sure it is worth solving
- Form an initial hypothesis
- Understand the current situation
- Uncover the complications
- Select a resolution that can be executed

Chapter Three: People Management

Whether you are in the business of manufacturing goods or providing services, people are your most important asset and require continual investment. Remarkable people managers are maniacally focused on hiring the right people, delegating effectively, and coaching for ongoing success and professional development.

Hire the best people for the target salary range

If you ever start to question the value of time spent recruiting and hiring new employees, simply recall your own experiences with a bad boss, coworker, or staff member. Such an individual, often unintentionally, leaves a wake of destruction in their path that impacts the entire organization. They devour time, energy, and morale.

To combat this risk, you need to be systematic about hiring the best people for the target salary range. This recommendation has two pieces. First, what does it mean to "hire the best people?" Very specifically, you need to start the hiring process by determining the single most important business objective the individual will be asked to achieve in the near term. If you are hiring a new product development manager and the principal objective is to release one new software product every six months, then hire a person with a proven track record of success and the skills needed for the job. The biggest mistakes that hiring managers make is hiring people based almost exclusively on either cultural fit or a general sense that an individual has a broad base of skills that could be used to take on most tasks. To be a great people manager, you instead need to focus on hiring people that will achieve overwhelming success on the specific business objective at hand.

The second piece of the recommendation "…for the target salary range" requires little explanation. If you have a one hundred thousand dollar budget for a position, you are not going to be able to hire Steve Jobs, Jack Welch, or Louis Gerstner. Make peace with this fact and move on.

Once you have determined the single most important business objective the new hire will be expected to achieve in the near term, the next step is to engineer away any hidden biases that you and your team have by identifying the "must-have" general skills and specialist skills that are required for success on the objective. These skills should be based on the attributes of star performers already in the role.

In the aforementioned new product development job, you might establish the following prioritized list of generalist skills:

Must have:
- Communication (especially with executives)
- Problem solving
- Leads through influence and with passion

Nice to have:
- Uses business judgment/Sees the big picture
- Cultural fit
- Negotiation
- Willing to challenge to get to the truth
- Able to synthesize mountains of information
- Time management
- Accountability

Prioritizing the list and sticking to your guns on the "must-have" skills is key. If candidates do not have the specific must-have skill, then do not hire them, as they are unlikely to succeed on their primary objective.

In addition to generalist skills, you must similarly prioritize the essential specialist skills. For the new product development job, you might prioritize as follows:

Must have:
- Client interviewing
- Ability to prioritize scope based on business merit
- People management

Nice to have:
- Technical skills such as programming
- Long range strategic planning
- Analytical ability
- Presentation skills

There is of course a fuzzy line between generalist skills and specialist skills. You do not need to get that classification precisely correct. What does matter is identifying the must have skills required for success on the candidate's primary business objective that allow you to make a go/no-go decision in an unbiased way. How many 'must-have' skills are required? The short answer is as many as you need to all but guarantee success on the business objective. At the same time, you do want to keep the list short enough so that you and your hiring team can evaluate the candidate practically during the interview process.

Once you have established the primary business objective for the job and the associated 'must-have' skills to ensure success, it is time to start interviewing. To do that, you are going to need a pipeline of qualified candidates. All great people managers continually cultivate a pipeline of potential future hires. In most circumstances, this can be done informally since hiring velocity is not rapid nor are potential candidates extremely difficult to find. In other circumstances, say Cirque de Soleil, finding a qualified candidate to fill the pipeline is like finding a needle in a haystack. According to a 2007 Wall Street Journal article, to fill its 500 new roles per year, Cirque de Soleil has "created a database of 20,000 potential performers. Among them: 24 giants (including a Ukrainian who is 8 foot 2), 23 whistlers, 466 contortionists, 14 pickpockets, 35 skateboarders, 1,278 clowns, eight dislocation artists and 73 people classified simply as small." If you do not have a sufficiently rich pipeline of your own, the next best source is referrals from other people within your organization. Outside recruiters and public job postings should be a last resort.

To build a strong candidate pool, you should look to the current star performers in similar roles within your company. By analyzing their background and how they came into your organization, you can establish a pattern and use it to target similar sources. Moreover, your current star performers are likely to be your best referral source for likeminded prospects.

Time spent recruiting and hiring the right people is the best investment an extremely skilled people manager can make. However, your time is still precious and should be used as effectively as possible. To make the best use of your time, prescreen candidates over the phone. Though you should never make a hiring decision over the phone, you should eliminate candidates for whom there is clearly no fit. The phone interview gives you an opportunity to learn about the candidate and for the candidate to learn about you. Since the most promising candidates have many attractive opportunities, you are selling to them as much as they are selling to you. The key information to look for during the phone screening interview is whether or not the candidate has had specific experience on the primary business objective that you are hiring for. What matters is what they have done, not what they would do. Encourage the interviewee to provide specific examples with concrete outcomes.

Once you have narrowed the field and have decided to bring in a small number of top candidates, you ought to interview as rigorously as possible. Make sure that your interviewing team clearly understands the primary business objective that the potential new hires will be responsible for. Remind the team to suppress their biases and to systematically test for the must-have generalist and specialist criteria required for success on that objective. Be direct with the interviewee by sharing the primary business goal. Ideally, the winning candidate should be able to vividly describe a specific instance in their employee where they accomplished the exact business objective you are hiring for. You can prompt for this insight by asking the candidate the question: "Tell me about a time when you..." In addition to testing for prior success on the primary business objective, you should validate – again with vivid actual detail – that the candidate possesses the must-have skills.

The best candidates have had prior overwhelming success on a similar primary business objective as well as all of the requisite skills. Sometimes, though it should be extremely rare, the business objective is so esoteric that you simply will not be able to source candidates with prior direct success. That is alright. However, you must immediately eliminate any candidate that does not possess every one of the must-have skills. An astute people manager is never deceived by the hope that the new hire can pick up the skill on the job. Let people pick up new skills on the job, but first make sure you hire only people that walk in the door with the right set of skills to be successful on their primary business objective.

Hiring well requires a comprehensive, team-based process. Final candidates should interview multiple times with multiple people. This ensures that the individual is looked at from different angles and will be a good overall fit on the team. The group consensus should always have the power to eliminate a candidate. However, the hiring manager must have the final say in a "yes" decision since they must believe in the person in order to be an effective coach and in order for the individual to be successful.

After you have interviewed a competitive set of candidates, it is time to make a hiring decision. If the decision feels hard, then you have probably not found the right person yet. Avoid hiring "the best of the rest." Many successful managers describe the decision to hire an individual with language evoking falling in love. When you interview the right person, you are going to feel it in your bones. Do not hire until your visceral response is "I must hire THIS person and not let them get away."

Some organizations, often the most flourishing ones, possess a core ideology that defines the corporate culture. The core ideology might be inward facing such as 'deliver the cutting edge of innovation' or 'provide unlimited growth and opportunities for employees.' Or, it may be outward facing such as 'bring happiness to the world' or 'improve the quality of human life.' Whatever it may be, the best way to maintain and enhance the strength of your ideology is to seek and hire people that already espouse the defining purpose. If this is the case, it should be one of the 'must-have' skills.

Zappos, the internet shoe and apparel retailer snapped up by Amazon for nearly $1 billion in stock, possesses the core ideology of providing the best customer service possible. The company internally calls this its WOW philosophy. New customer service representatives are put through and intensive four-week indoctrination in the company's strategies, culture, and customer engagement practices. At some point during this period, the company actually makes people an offer to quit! In addition to their full salary from time served, the company offers employees $1000 to leave. The obvious rationale is to have individuals weed themselves out when they are not a cultural fit.

Delegate effectively

Poor managers fall into one of two camps - those who under-delegate and those who over-delegate. Most managers land in their position of authority by being outstanding individual contributors. They often hold the belief that no one in the world can do what they do faster or better. This attribute tends to make new managers atrocious under-delegators, who hand off only low risk tasks since they do not possess sufficient trust in their staff. Although new managers are canny enough to realize they must delegate to be successful, their fear of their team's possible underperformance prevents them from doing so.

By contrast, the over-delegators, overwhelmed with their new responsibilities, hand over projects that exceed a staff member's motivation or ability. The pressures of the managerial role override their do-it-yourself individual contributor mentality before they have learned the art of more restrained delegation.

The most essential skill in being a judicious delegator is being able to clearly define the concrete, measureable objectives associated with a given task or workstream. Share this objective with the individual you are delegating to by communicating to them what success looks like. The objective not only gives the individual a clear compass to sail by, but also gives them an unambiguous way to know when they are done.

As you formulate your objective, you should also think about the skills required for success. In almost all circumstances, you should delegate to individuals that already have the requisite skills to complete the task. Delegating is different from coaching. Delegating is about efficient use of your time and about success on your projects. In contrast, coaching aims to help your staff grow by introducing new responsibilities. Coaching involves a significant and worthy investment of time on the part of you and your staff. Both have value and as a perceptive manager you need to strike a balance between tasks that should be delegated and tasks that should be used for coaching.

Once you have formulated the objective and selected the skilled individual, you need to hand off the task in a way that all but guarantees success. First, provide as much information as you have and guidance on how to find missing information. Second, answer any questions that the person has about the task. Third, have the individual play back his or her understanding of the task to make sure it is fully understood. Though one of the most important parts of successful delegation, this is also the piece most frequently forgotten. Last, agree to a deadline for completion that provides adequate time for success. In larger projects, you may also need to agree on milestones or to require a written progress plan.

Detailed step-by-step guidance is intentionally missing from the hand off process just described. If the person needs to be micro-managed, then he or she is the wrong individual to whom to delegate. Moreover, working out step-by-step instructions is a poor use of your time. By being flexible in the process, you are showing trust in your staff; but, remember, though flexible in the process, be fixed in the result.

Once you have delegated the task, make yourself accessible to answer questions and to provide guidance. Depending on the scope, duration, and importance of the task, you should monitor progress toward the objective to ensure success by the deadline. Finally, remember that whoever does the task, it remains your responsibility as a manager if things go wrong. By giving credit and taking blame, you maintain accountability and build trust.

With highly motivated and highly skilled employees, you will reach the nirvana of delegation – the ability to 'fire and forget.' With such individuals, you will be able to lengthen the time between check-ins, as they are likely to be more expert than you are at a particular task or work-stream. Still, employ two mechanisms at your disposal to assess the quality of the work. One way of doing this performance 'audit' is dig a couple of deep wells. In accounting, this is the equivalent of counting every unit of a single type of product in inventory.

The other way is to sniff test at the macro level. Again, in the accounting world, this is comparable to making sure that there is at least one box of every type of product in inventory.

Coach for ongoing success and professional development

Coaching is a close cousin of delegation but with a key difference. In both delegation and coaching, great managers must define clear, concrete objectives. However, effective delegation hinges on transferring tasks to individuals that already possess the requisite skills for success. When you are in coaching mode, you need to invest time and energy since you are going into the situation knowing that the individual needs to develop a new set of skills.

The fundamental secret of being a great coach is tailoring everything, absolutely everything, to the person and to the task. This personalization philosophy extends from the skills you identify to work on together to the style you utilize in providing feedback, and everything in between.

The most common mistake that managers make both consciously and unconsciously is projecting their own professional desires onto their staff. In their defense, they are following admirably the Golden Rule of doing unto others as you would have done unto you. However, a better rule in coaching is to do unto others as they would have done unto themselves, a powerful update to the Golden Rule that transcends the world of coaching. Though you are on a general management track, many of your employees may wish to remain on a functional track at this phase in their career. Talk to people to understand who they want to become and what their motivations are.

Great coaches understand that their employees possess strengths, latent skills, and weaknesses. Consider a baseball player early in his career who is a good hitter and right fielder, a terrible pitcher, and an unproven first baseman. In this instance, it is fairly obvious that the player should maximize time spent with the batting coach and minimize time spent with the pitching coach. That is the only way to manufacture the next Babe Ruth. Though everyone sees the truth in the baseball analogy, many managers in the business world spend their time identifying weaknesses and then toiling futilely to improve them, a criminal waste of everyone's time.

Instead, be a shrewd coach by spending eighty percent of your time identifying strengths and helping people become more of who they already are. Here is what to do with the other twenty percent: dip into the pool of latent skills and test for aptitude. It will become apparent very quickly if the latent ability can be developed into a strength. If it is not a strength, toss it in the weakness bucket, cut bait and do not look back. There are a million treasures hiding in the pool of latent skills and they are generally easy to uncover.

Identifying strengths to build on and latent skills to develop is not a solitary managerial activity. Since you cannot be there all the time, the individual must be fully invested in his or her own development. Because people are most successful in personal and professional growth when they have identified for themselves the skills they want to build, do not automatically project your own strengths or the traits you want to develop onto others. Though employees often have a good idea of their strengths, you can be an effective partner with them in selecting latent skills to develop that they are passionate about and that will build their career.

Inspirational coaching requires empathy. Every human being has both a deep rooted need to feel vital and a deep rooted fear of criticism. The feeling of importance is one of the foundations of self-confidence and should be nurtured. True, in the process of coaching, you will routinely give both positive and negative feedback. To remain a nurturing coach, then, in every interaction, strive to have the positive feedback outweigh the negative, preferably leading with the reassuring. Avoid being heavy-handed with the initial positive comments; do not insult your employee's intelligence. But understand that this requisite spoonful of sugar, if genuinely felt and expressed, will keep any ensuing criticism constructive.

Remember to be as specific, sincere, and concise as possible in your feedback. Simply saying "You did a great job" is flattery, not feedback. Such non-specific praise will not have its intended effect even if you mean every vague word of it. Instead, provide details of what was done well and why it was important to you or to the organization. For example, tell the individual "You did a great job on the analysis of last month's capacity utilization. The data showed that we need to accelerate the addition of new capital equipment to meet demand."

When providing constructive comments, you also need to be more Socratic rather than didactic. This means having an open and enlightening conversation that eventually shows how you would have performed the assigned task, rather than simply announcing the information by terse decree. Although the latter is a tantalizing time-saver, remember the dictates of real coaching require the former.

In addition to feeling indispensable (or nearly) and talked to (not at), your employees generally wish to be independent. It is a source of pride for them. Thus, for many, being coached may feel like being micromanaged. To avoid ill-will, you must be as transparent as possible. Coaching is not meant to be a stealth activity; let the individual know when you are in coaching mode. Though it may be obvious to you, it will not be to your employees, as they generally will expect you to be in delegation mode. You should tell the person which skill you are coaching and remind them that your goal is his or her professional development. While it is possible to always be coaching, avoid the temptation. After a person receives criticism, even the constructive kind, his or her self-confidence takes one step back. Give the person time to heal and to independently take two steps forward.

In general, people prefer and derive the greatest benefit from immediate feedback. However, in some circumstances, people may grow more effectively with delayed feedback so it is a good idea to confirm the person's preference. If they express no preference, opt for the immediate approach.

Either way, a great framework for providing feedback is the "Build On… / Think About…" method. For example, if a person is giving a presentation, take a sheet of paper and make two columns. On the top left, write "Build On…". On the top right, write "Think About.." During the presentation, capture positive feedback in the "Build On" section and constructive criticism or open action items in the "Think About" section. Again, strive to have the positive outweigh the negative. At the end of the presentation, hand the feedback form to the individual. Avoid the temptation to make copies since coaching is a gift to the individual and should not have the emotional baggage of a performance evaluation. Great coaches that adopt this method use it in every interaction. Occasionally, and only if warranted, fill in only positive feedback. This well-earned reward gives the feeling of getting a report card with straight A's.

Not only do employees need real time comments, they also need to understand their trajectory on skill building over time. To accommodate this requirement, great managers schedule comprehensive feedback conversations at intervals of no shorter than two months and no longer than six months. These sessions should be independent of any formal performance evaluation tied to compensation or promotion. If your organization has the capacity, provide the individual with 360 degree feedback every six months. During the gathering of 360 degree feedback, the manager should interview the individual's subordinates, peers, and superiors to gain insight on how well the person is building the specific skills on which you are coaching.

Only keep your A-players

To be a great manager, you have to have a great team. Though painful for you and for underperforming staff members, you must remove and replace underperforming individuals. This is a reality during a period of layoffs as well as during a period of normal business operation.

During a layoff, euphemistically referred to as a 'reduction-in-force', just remember that your mission is to keep your A-players. When deciding between two individuals, keep the stronger current performer. Often managers will fall into the trap of retaining the wrong person for purely emotional reasons. Avoid the following rationalizations:

- "We owe him"
- "It is my fault as a manager that she is not succeeding… I just need more time to coach her"
- "He is new…"

Even during the normal course of business, you have a managerial duty to optimize your team's performance. The damage from a B- player (or worse) is widespread. Your precious time as a manager will be drained. The other members of your staff will be de-motivated or even directly negatively affected by an underperforming peer. Additionally, underperformers are under constant personal strain. Though the immediate transition period will be painful for them, the individual has a right to be happy in the long term by becoming an A-player on another team inside your company or beyond. If you have been providing periodic effective feedback, it should not be a surprise to the individuals being managed out. They should have adequate time to pursue other opportunities.

Recap

Here are the concepts you can immediately apply to be a great people manager:
- Hire the best people for the target salary range
- Delegate effectively
- Coach for ongoing success and professional development
- Keep only your A-players

Chapter Four: Change Management

When I was nearing the completion of my Masters degree in electrical engineering, I had to make a major life choice about which direction to take my career. I wanted to apply my creativity to improve the lives of other people and I found that opportunity with an innovative semiconductor company in Silicon Valley. This company made chips that could be reconfigured by customers to work in equipment ranging from big iron Internet Routers to cutting edge consumer electronics. Better still, this company was the only one on the planet attempting to build a new product using the precise (and very esoteric) technology that I focused on during graduate school. The stars were aligned and I was on Cloud Nine.

From the title of this chapter, you are probably beginning to guess what happened next. Six months into my tenure as a junior product developer, the company terminated the project and took a $5 million write-down for in-process research and development. Fortunately, it was the late 1990's, and the organization was growing by leaps and bounds; there were still jobs for all of us. This was my first exposure to an endless string of reorganizations, mergers, divestitures, and new initiatives. In short, it was my first exposure to an endless string of change, which I soon learned was the only constant.

In that first project termination, I felt the rug had been pulled out from beneath me. The technology on which I invested years of blood, sweat, and tears would likely never see the light of day. I briefly feared and distrusted change and nearly signed my soul over to a parking lot headhunter (at the time, headhunters would wait in parking lots trying to recruit anything that moved). However, after a few sleepless nights and many conversations with my supportive wife, I began to view change as opportunity. During the remainder of my career, I have found that the greatest opportunities for rapid professional development and financial growth occur during periods of disruptive change.

As you move from being a great individual contributor to being a great manager, you will shift from being changed to leading change. To be effective, you must embrace the memory of how challenging your first exposure to corporate upheaval was. Draw upon those lessons to guide your team when instituting new initiatives. In the change management framework explored below, you will see that the common thread in fluid change management is empathetically addressing the needs of behaviorally irrational human beings — in other words, people just like you.

Challenge the status quo with a new, positive vision

Getting people to change is hard work. To give you the best odds of becoming a great change manager, it helps to understand the work that earned Amos Tversky and Daniel Kahneman their Nobel Prize in 2002 for pioneering work in behavioral economics. In a nutshell, Tversky and Kahneman reasoned that people faced with choices involving gains are risk averse and that people faced with choices involving losses are risk loving. In fact, the professors noted that merely framing a logically identical choice as a loss (of lives, of money, etc.) rather than a foregone gain induces most of the human race to take large if not extraordinary risks.

So, how does all this tie back to change management? As a change leader, your job is to inspire people to take action that will by definition move them from their comfortable status quo. If you understand the human propensity for loss aversion, then you realize you have two choices: either to create a 'burning platform' or to establish a sense of urgency and motivate people to change.

The first choice is to create a 'burning platform.' For example, you can vividly paint of picture of an external threat to your organization which they will logically tie to loss of their own job security. To be effective, individuals must have either underappreciated the severity of the threat or better yet had no prior knowledge of its existence.

Being able to draw attention to the burning platform from which you are speaking will make you a good change manager, but not a great one. If you look around, you will find that its use is pervasive. Motivating people with fear to avoid a loss will get them moving, and fast. However, the quick rush out of the gate carries the expected consequence that the energy behind your change initiative will not last. Thus, limit use of a burning platform to those instances when you need immediate change on an initiative that is short term and low in complexity.

It is far more effective to inspire people with hope than to motivate them with fear. That brings us to the second, superior choice, to establish a sense of urgency for a change initiative. In many loss aversion studies, researchers determined that people require gains to be a factor of two larger than a possible loss. For example, in order to bet and potentially lose $20, Kahneman and Tversky found that people on average require a potential payoff of $40. As a tenacious change manager, this means that, yes, you will need to work twice as hard to paint a positive vision of the future strong enough to induce people to risk their status quo. But, if you succeed, the return is enormous since you will provide nearly limitless fuel to sustain your change initiative.

To accept and ultimately embrace change, people need to motivate themselves on both a rational and emotional level. To appeal to the rational 'left brain', your vision should feel achievable and should provide a personal, tangible benefit. Providing a compelling set of facts is a persuasive way to speak to the rational mind.

Seasoned change managers know that rational appeals are only half the battle. To drive successful change, you must also speak to the emotional right brain. The best technique to accomplish that is through storytelling – for example, by creating a vibrant, positive picture of the future. Additionally, you should strive to connect your change initiative to the deep needs of individuals. Though self-interest is a strong motivator, the most powerful approach you can take is sincerely helping people feel they are making the world a better place for themselves, their friends and family, and mankind as a whole.

All this may sound a bit hokey, but you should be able to identify a higher purpose in nearly every professional. In some professions, like medicine and teaching, the higher purpose is obvious. In others, perhaps financial services and consulting, you may have to ask 'why is that important?' a few times, but eventually you will get there.

Communicating your new, positive vision that challenges the status quo and inspires change is as important as crafting that vision in the first place. Words alone will not do. You must also show your own commitment to change through your every deed. For starters, a useful best practice is to create a guiding coalition that includes individuals with high positional authority, expertise, and credibility. After all, if the influencers inside your organization do not support your change initiative, then it is doomed before you even start.

Engineer the environment for success

All change initiatives, especially large ones, require careful planning. To engineer the environment for success, you must plan your actions and plan your resources.

Think of building your action plan the way you would build a business plan for a startup company. The key is to script the critical moves with clear, specific direction. This does not mean that you personally need to lead every critical work-stream. Nor does it mean that you need to plan out every step involved. Rather, your mission is to articulate the end vision of what great looks like and to define the crucial milestones along the way. To be a resourceful change manager on large initiatives, you will routinely share and even transfer responsibility. Remember, however, that even though you are sharing leadership, you always retain final accountability.

The actions that truly matter are the ones that require people to do their work differently. To find those actions, you must interview people that are already realizing your end vision. If they do not exist inside your company, go find them in the larger world. Authors Chip and Dan Heath of *Switch: How to Change Things When Change Is Hard* refer to these people as bright spots. Those individuals and their stories will illuminate the way for others.

Excellent change managers know that little happens by accident. They do not wait for the welcome, unexpected blue bird to land on their shoulder. Instead, they maniacally plan for, generate, and publicize short term wins. This is so important, it bears repeating. Great change managers maniacally plan for, generate, and publicize short term wins. These wins must be unambiguous and directly related to the change effort. By sharing short term wins, you fuel the change effort by showing people that their actions are having an immediate payoff. Assume that people are looking for any reason to jump ship and return to the old status quo; your job is to provide real hope that the tropical island paradise lies just over the horizon.

In addition to action planning, the second component of engineering the environment for success is resource planning. The most obvious feature of this is securing the necessary people, technology, and capital. That is the rational part. As with all elements of change management, there is an emotional component of resource planning. Specifically, great change managers empower broad based action by identifying and systematically removing obstacles to success. At the very least, this will require a careful examination of the processes resident in your organization that may be inconsistent with your vision of the future.

These processes will run the gamut from operations to finance to human resources. For example, if you are an internet retailer and your mission is to transform your customer service, there are many processes that can stand in the way. Do you employ a drop ship model where you receive orders from customers and then forward them to possibly unreliable producers who subsequently directly ship to customers? Is your focus on inventory turns causing you to leave customers frustrated with 'item sold out' messages? Are you measuring your customer service professionals on calls handled per minute, forcing them to be curt with customers?

Processes are one resource planning obstacle to success. A second is encouraging people to become more risk taking. Your inspiring, positive vision of the future is a piece of the puzzle. As a great change manager, you will need to align and upgrade the skills of people in the organization to make them comfortable with risk. Again, stories will be a key ally. Nordstrom teems with stories (some true and some urban legend) about sales clerks accepting returns for heavily worn items or items sold by other stores. FedEx and UPS share innumerable stories about package deliveries in extreme conditions. What are your stories of risk taking that align with your change initiative? Find them and shout them from the rooftops.

Returning to the analogy of the startup business plan, you should engineer but not over-engineer for success. Carve out as much time as you can for planning, focusing on the key actions and resources that matter, then execute and iterate. Your plans should remain adaptable to account for the unpredictability of people, technology, and processes.

Make change stick

If you have challenged the status quo with a positive vision and engineered the actions and resources for success, then you are two thirds of the way to being a great change manager. The last requirement is that you master the ability to make change stick.

The most basic way to do this is to periodically remind people of what has already been accomplished. Think of this as an aggregation of the short terms wins that you publicized into a larger picture. It should be a picture that shows where you started, how far you have come, and how much further everyone needs to travel to realize the end goal.

As you probably guessed, there is a deeper emotional requirement here too. Your mission is no less than to upgrade people's individual identity in a way that anchors new approaches in the culture. For example, 'I am a hospitality professional that provides people with a clean, comfortable room to sleep in and I work for a company that provides a home away from home.' Or, 'I am a consultant that helps people become more productive and I work for a firm that helps productive people to provide a higher standard of living for their families." The stickiest change builds and reinforces noble purpose at a personal and emotional level.

Recap

To excel, you not only must conceive major initiatives but also must architect and continually fuel initiatives for success. Here are the concepts you can immediately apply to be a great change manager:
* Challenge the status quo with a new, positive vision
* Engineer the environment for success
* Make change stick

Chapter Five: Crisis Management

When most people hear the words 'crisis management', they most often think of dramatic corporate disasters such as the BP oil spill, Toyota's accelerator pedal recall, or the Chicago Tylenol murders. For most of us, these infrequent events catch our attention but do not affect our everyday lives. Instead, individuals face a constant barrage of professional crises that must be managed. At the very least, these situations increase stress and reduce happiness. In the extreme, they threaten your career.

One of the most impressive and consistent characteristics among senior leaders is how calm they seem despite the enormous responsibilities and the political pressure that surrounds them. You want to be the one that other people want in the foxhole with them when the bombs start flying. Your ability to remain, or to appear to remain, calm under fire will define you as an unflappable crisis manager.

Johnson & Johnson's handling of the Chicago area Tylenol poisonings is widely regarded as the best example of corporate crisis management. Let's look at their actions to extract best practices that you can apply to your everyday crises.

On Wednesday September 29, 1982, 12-year-old Mary Kellerman of Elk Grove Village, Illinois died a few hours after taking one Extra-Strength Tylenol to treat her cold symptoms. Doctors initially attributed her death to a stroke. The same morning, Adam Janus of Arlington Heights, Illinois took a Tylenol to sooth his mild chest pain. Within hours he was dead of what doctors suspected to be a massive heart attack. That evening, Adam's brother and sister-in-law consumed capsules from the same Tylenol bottle while gathering to mourn. They met a similar fate. Dr. Thomas Kim of the Northwest Community Hospital suspected that the deaths of the three Janus family members were linked, but his hypothesis was exposure to poison gas.

On a typical day in the Chicago metropolitan area about 200 people die of natural and unnatural causes. So, identifying any common thread between the deaths of Mary Kellerman and the three Janus family members amounts to finding a needle in a haystack. However, two off-duty firefighters did just that and at lightning speed.

Knowing that young Mary Kellerman had taken Tylenol before her death, Elk Grove firefighter Richard Keyworth asked his friend Arlington Heights firefighter Philip Cappitelli to check with paramedics to see if the Janus family members had also ingested the pain reliever. Once the connection was found, police retrieved the suspicious bottles from the Kellerman and Janus homes and sent them for testing.

By Thursday September 30, Cook County Chief Toxicologist Michael Shaffer confirmed that capsules in the bottles were filled with approximately 65 milligrams of potassium cyanide, about 10,000 times the dose necessary to kill the average person. Johnson and Johnson was notified immediately and Chicago police officers drove through the streets blasting warnings through their loudspeakers urging people to avoid taking Tylenol. All three major television networks reported the story in the evening news.

On Friday October 1st, the Food and Drug Administration issued a consumer advisory to avoid taking Tylenol capsules "until the series of deaths in the Chicago area can be clarified." Despite the warnings, three more people perished from tainted Tylenol in the Chicago area by the end of the day bringing the death toll to seven.

In the ensuing chaos, Tylenol took as much time as they could to analyze the facts. They discovered that the deadly bottles had come from four manufacturing lots produced at two separate factories over the period of many weeks. Though cyanide was available at the factories, the company concluded that the bottles must have been tainted after shipping since the deaths were concentrated in one geographic area and in a short time span. The evidence pointed to the hypothesis that someone must have purchased the bottles, added the poison, and put the bottles back on the shelf. (Though a conviction has never been obtained, the prime suspect served 13 years of a 20 year sentence for attempting to extort $1 million from Johnson and Johnson as well as six unrelated counts of mail and credit card fraud).

Johnson and Johnson had taken the time to establish the root cause and considered their next move. On Tuesday October 5, the company halted production and advertising and issued a nationwide recall of 31 million bottles with a retail value of over $100 million. After extensive testing, investigators found a total of seven bottles with between three and ten tainted capsules placed in six Chicago area stores.

In the aftermath, Tylenol's share of the pain reliever market dropped from 35 percent to 8 percent. Respected industry pundits confidently pronounced that the Tylenol brand could never recover. Against this headwind, Johnson and Johnson reintroduced Tylenol a mere five weeks later on November 11, 1982 with new tamper proof packaging, a large advertising campaign, and a $2.50 coupon. Within a year, Tylenol had regained the entire share it had lost. As of this writing, Tylenol remains a household name and is likely sitting in your medicine cabinet.

Give yourself as much space and time as possible

A crisis is a crisis because you are faced with a threat or opportunity and not enough time to make a clear, fact-based decision. Everyday crises include being confronted by a co-worker, making a keep-or-kill choice on a project, and managing work-life balance. Whether the crisis is actual or perceived, the stress is palpable. Under such strain, the worst blunder you can make is to execute without a sufficient knowledge.

The only way to gain a fact base is to carve out as much space and time as possible to diagnose the situation. In extreme situations, you should at least have the ability to step out of the room and collect your thoughts. Most often, you will have hours and even days to act. When carving out time, remember your mission is to resolve the crisis to the best of your ability the first time, not to solve it as fast as possible at all costs.

On Thursday September 30th, Johnson and Johnson learned that the company was facing an epic corporate and public health crisis. Rather than make an immediate defensive and emotional reaction, the company took five days to fig-ure out what to do with the product on the shelves and five weeks to figure out how to re-launch the brand. By taking as much time as they could to determine the facts and craft a decisive response, Johnson and Johnson established the model of what great looks like in crisis management.

Apply your rational rather than emotional problem solving skills to the crisis

Although you will be facing a compressed time scale, apply your full set of problem solving skills to the crisis. Form an initial hypothesis, gather facts, identify complications, and choose a resolution. When crisis strikes, the most important and oft ignored part of problem solving is fact gathering. Take a deep breath, remove the emotion, and try to identify the true root of the prob-lem. Make a fact based decision, not a gut decision.

In my experience, most professional crises come in the form of interpersonal conflict. To solve this form of crisis, you need to get into the head of the other person and know how they want the crisis to end. Though you may have interpreted their actions as a direct attack, much of the time the other person's motivations have little or nothing to do with you.

Unfortunately, there are times when a fellow coworker really is out to get you. Though this happens less frequently than you perceive, the recommended course of action is fortunately the same. As long as you are physically safe, hunker down and do your job to the best of your ability. By spending all his or her effort on unproductive machinations, your nemesis will ultimately be out of a job. Moreover, by excelling at your work, you will lower your stress since you will not have time to think about the other person.

Recap

If you remain calm when faced with a crisis, you will be able to bring an effective resolution with a minimum of both effort and drama. Here are the concepts you can immediately apply to be a great crisis manager:
- Give yourself as much space and time as possible
- Apply your rational rather than emotional problem solving skills to the crisis

Chapter Six: Taking Charge

After four years digesting a prior acquisition, my employer decided to expand into an adjacent market space. Though I learned many great lessons in the days leading up to the deal's close, none was more powerful than the education I received watching one of my peers artfully take charge of the first due diligence meeting. By commandeering that first meeting, he set himself up as a leader of the acquisition and the subsequent integration process. In short, he showed what great looks like in taking charge.

Allow me to paint a more detailed picture for you. Ten functional leads representing product management, human resources, finance, legal, and other areas assembled for a top secret meeting in a windowless basement conference room. All of us had signed non-disclosure agreements and all of us had roughly equivalent positional authority. Eight of the ten people in the room, including me, came in bright-eyed and bushy-tailed and just thrilled that we had been chosen by our CEO to contribute our functional expertise to the vetting process. The other two, however, had larger appetites. They were vying to supercharge their careers by taking leadership of the overall acquisition. Our CEO, known for his skill at identifying and developing talent, clearly put these two exceptional individuals into a competitive situation to test their mettle.

One of the two, let's call him Jason, emerged as the clear victor. Here is what he did.

Pre-syndicate your ideas with key players
BEFORE you get to the meeting

Jason had actually won long before he ever set foot in the room. Well before the meeting, Jason prioritized the level of influence of the people that would be in the meeting. He then individually met with each of the key players to deeply understand their hopes and concerns and to share his own thoughts. Jason's objective was not to win them over to his side. Rather, his objective was to integrate their ideas with his own to build a coherent vision.

This one technique, pre-syndication, is hands down the single most powerful way to take charge. Despite its obviousness, few people actually use it, enabling you to distance yourself from the crowd simply by being one of those diligent few. In my experience, most people have never even thought of systematically pre-syndicating their ideas. Among those that know it is good for their health, few actually take time to schedule and execute a round of pre-syndication. It is hard work and requires meticulous planning, but will yield enormous rewards.

Starting today, you must make it your practice to pre-syndicate ideas with the key influencers and decision makers that will be in your meetings. You should make it your objective that you will never be surprised in a meeting. You should make it your aim that you always walk into meetings with reasonable certainty that the decision has <u>already</u> been made. That is what elevates good to great.

Arrive early and claim the physical position of leadership

Being a person that is conditioned to arrive early, I was there to observe Jason walk into the room a good five to ten minutes before the scheduled meeting start time. I watched closely as Jason's eyes purposefully sized up the environment. Though this was a room in which tables and chairs were constantly reconfigured by beings unknown, there is a clear front of the room with whiteboards and flip charts. Jason positioned himself at the front of the room, nearest the whiteboard. He staked his claim by setting his belongings down at the head of a rectangular table and only then engaged me in conversation. Where appropriate, and if you have enough time, you can even reconfigure the room to your advantage.

You may think this sort of thing is beneath you as a leader. Your intellect and abilities, after all, should speak for themselves and you should not have to resort to 'gimmicks' like jockeying for where you sit in a room. Although logically sound, that pride will hold you back from taking charge.

Unless your seniority trumps everyone else's in the room, it is a bold move to sit at the head of a rectangular table. Most people, possibly trying to be respectful in the event that a more senior person arrives, will choose a seat on one of the long sides of a rectangular table. We were conditioned this way as children sitting down for family meals.

By arriving early, Jason set himself up for success in two ways. As mentioned, he placed himself in the physical position of authority in the room. Second, Jason had time to establish rapport with each individual as they entered the room. When the meeting started, he was calm, confident, and collected.

Control the group agenda and goals

Controlling a meeting extends beyond the more generic, but still important, topic of meeting effectiveness (covered in a separate chapter). To own a meeting, you must set the agenda, prioritize the group's goals, and get buy-in to next steps at the conclusion. All of this requires careful planning.

Though it will greatly enhance your likelihood of controlling the meeting, being the first one to speak does not guarantee success. In more chaotic situations among equals, it pays to wait and then enter as the person that brings structure. This is exactly what Jason did. He was quiet but listening carefully at the beginning of the acquisition kick-off meeting. His (in retrospect) competitor spoke first, providing background information on the target company rather than beginning by setting the agenda. Jason's adversary committed a crucial error. He fell into the trap of believing that his superior knowledge by itself would allow him to take charge. As the conversation began to drift among various participants, Jason stepped in and began to organize the group. While his challenger lost steam after a quick jump out of the gate, Jason gradually gained momentum.

Secure the commitment of everyone involved

During the course of the meeting, Jason sensed that the tide was turning his way. However, he needed to be absolutely sure. Though the mechanism to secure commitment varies from situation to situation, the most effective method in a business meeting is to be the individual that obtains agreement on next steps.

Inspire with a positive vision of the future

Every great performance has a central theme at its core. This is as true in a corporate environment as it is in the theater. In business settings, the person whom others ultimately allow to take charge bears the responsibility of inspiring the team with a positive vision of the future.

Jason's final flourish, which cemented him as the team leader, was to paint of picture of how the combined organization would benefit our customers, our employees, and our shareholders.

Recap

When I shared this taking charge framework with an attorney with whom I work, he smiled immediately. Curious, I asked him whether his was a skeptical smile of disagreement. He answered, "Just the opposite. In the law, we have an expression for this: 'control the document.'" So, if you want to become great at taking charge, you must plan carefully to 'control the document': both the physical and intellectual resources that will define the outcome.

Here are the concepts you can immediately apply to become great at taking charge:
* Pre-syndicate your ideas with key players BEFORE you get to the meeting
* Arrive early and claim the physical position of leadership
* Control the group agenda and goals
* Secure the commitment of everyone involved
* Inspire with a positive vision of the future

Chapter Seven: Corporate Culture

I once read a book that argued corporate culture cannot be created; it develops organically as a consequence of consistent behaviors. My immediate reaction was that this statement is dangerously naïve. Beware of statements that sound completely true merely because they include a fundamental truth within. It is true that culture is created by and sustained by consistent deeds. However, it is patently false that corporate culture cannot be created. Good cultures can develop on their own. Great cultures must be built and continuously nurtured.

Choose your focused cultural identity

Most companies have good corporate cultures. They have to almost by definition. If you consistently treat your customers, suppliers, shareholders, and employees poorly, then you will not have a company for very long. Yet many firms have only an ethereal identity. They espouse and generally do live by a credo of commitment to their various constituencies. However, the companies cannot be pinned down for focus on any one area. When a new and worthy value comes along, such as corporate social responsibility, good cultures add it as another ingredient to the brew.

Great companies choose their cultural identity with the same discipline that they use to build long term business strategy. The most successful business strategies employ focus that often involves tradeoffs. Truly well-constructed strategies rely on a unique strength of your organization, thereby providing some defense against the competition. Classic business strategy tradeoffs are things like speed versus accuracy, cost versus service, innovation versus consistency (I acknowledge there is an efficient frontier on these tradeoff dimensions; for example, for a given cost structure, companies need to choose the best level of service possible.)

Cultures with focus enjoy two benefits. First, a focused culture accelerates decision making. For example, if your environment has an employee-focused culture, then you will hold on to employees longer during tough economic times than if your environment were profit-focused. You would also add employee capacity more slowly during strong economic times. Second, a focused culture signals to your stakeholders why you make the decisions that you do. When you are cost focused, passengers on your low cost airline will understand why you have not yet replaced the green shag carpeting and the disco ball. They come to you with expectations of cheap and safe. Being focused will force you to remain consistent since your stakeholders will call you to the carpet on incompatible actions.

There are an infinite variety of focused cultures. The four most common include:
- Customer focus: mantra = delight your customers (examples: Zappos, Nordstrom)
- Employee focus: mantra = provide long term growth and security for your employees (examples: academic institutions of today and UPS of old)
- Innovation focus: mantra = wow! (examples: Apple, 3M)
- Profit (or cost) focus; mantra = money is what matters (examples: Southwest Airlines, most financial institutions)
- Social focus: mantra = promote the public interest (examples: not-for-profits and L3C's - low-profit limited liability companies)

There is nothing inherently right or wrong about any of these cultures. Even profit focused cultures can consistently do great things for their employees, customers, suppliers, and shareholders. The point is that when they hire, when they fund innovation, when they define customer service processes, when they reupholster airplane seats, they make their decisions on the basis of profit maximization.

Drive total consistency of culture across your organization

To thrive, your focused cultural identity must be consistent across every business process. This consistency should exist first and foremost in deeds and only secondarily in words. Anyone can adopt noble words. Enron's mission statement was "Respect, Integrity, Communication and Excellence." Words without actions are empty.

If you are an innovation-focused company, for example, there are a million ways to drive consistency. Do you hire creative people and then provide insufficient incentives to reward them for their intellectual contributions? Do you launch innovative new software products while allowing portions of your portfolio to languish? Your innovation culture must be ingrained across operations, human resources, finance, new product development, and so on.

Build an ever expanding story library

The most effective way to develop and sustain your focused corporate culture is by building an ever expanding story library. Your employees will want to be the protagonists of these narratives and will endeavor to make that happen. Just think of the last time your CEO told a story of excellence at an all-company meeting. Part of you felt inspired while the other part felt jealous that the story was not about you. Compelling anecdotes that reinforce your culture are created every day. They are all around you; you just have to discover and retell them. Since stories are perhaps the most effective means of communication, once retold they have the potential to inspire both employees and customers.

Stories have a limited lifespan and are prone to distortion over time. To get the most out of them, you should reveal your best stories in a publically accessible format, thus extending their life and making them less prone to distortion. Be careful, though: an old story is just that – old. People invariably will ask "Yeah, but what you have done for me lately?" To keep your identity alive, continually expand your story library.

As you add to your story library, quality trumps quantity and focus trumps variety. You do not need a million anecdotes about employees rowing through flooded streets to deliver an overnight package before the 12 pm deadline. You need one resonant yarn. Additionally, take care that the stories you select unambiguously reinforce your focused identity. If your focus is customer service, then a story about an employee who saved $10 million dollars by centralizing purchasing is simply not on point.

Teach everyone to challenge ideas, not people

One of the most enlightening conversations that I ever had was with an entrepreneur who had recently sold his company to a much larger competitor. I had worked with him and with many of his employees and was immediately struck by their creativity and collaboration. So, I asked him what he did to build the culture at his company. His answer was "I taught everyone to challenge ideas, not people." Imagine if your company operated that way.

Embedding this ideal within your culture begins, of course, with your own behavior. However, you do have more work to do. Subtle and not so subtle infighting is a natural, albeit degenerative, state for nearly every organization. If your company is to rise to this ideal, you must make it clear in actions that personal attacks are unacceptable. At minimum, you must call people out on such behavior when you observe it. If necessary, you may need to terminate an employee regardless of their performance if they do not share this ideal. Remember to reward and provide highly visible recognition for those that do.

Recap

Even if you do not invest any effort beyond operating legally and ethically, your organization will organically develop a good corporate culture. It will have elements of innovation, customer focus, employee focus, social responsibility, etc. However, if you want to create and sustain a truly great culture, here are the concepts you can immediately apply:
- Choose your focused cultural identity
- Drive total consistency of culture across your organization
- Build an ever expanding story library
- Teach everyone to challenge ideas, not people

Chapter Eight: Meetings That Matter

If you are already a manager, or are about to become one, then odds are that you will be spending most of the rest of your life huddled in physical or virtual meetings. You have an obligation to engineer your meetings for success regardless of the topic at hand. To become respected as a person that runs meetings that matter, you should optimize what happens before, during, and after the meeting.

Pre-syndicate your ideas with key players BEFORE you get to the meeting

As discussed in the chapter on "Taking Charge", you must make it your practice to pre-syndicate ideas with the key influencers and decision makers that will be in your meetings. Yes, this does mean that you will enter the realm of the ridiculous with meetings about meetings. But, elieve me, it is time well spent since you will achieve the goal of always walking into a meeting where you have reasonable certainty regarding the outcome. The amount of time that you spend on this process, of course, depends on the magnitude of the decision at hand and on the amount of time that you and your team have.

There will be times when key decision makers are simply not available. When that happens, it pays to spend time thinking about how they will react in your meeting. Start by understanding their root motivations. Those motivations will typically be tied to both personal objectives and business objectives, so make sure to explore both. Once you frame their motivations, someone on your team should role play the individual and poke as many holes as possible in your pitch. Though you will not be able to defend against an armor piercing bullet, you can at least sleep well the night before in Kevlar pajamas.

Start and end your meetings on time

Advice to start and end your meetings on time may seem too obvious to commit to ink and paper. However, ask yourself when the last time was that you actually attended a meeting that met this objective. In my experience, most meetings start five or ten minutes late and run over by the same amount.

By starting meetings on time, you show respect for the participants. You will rapidly develop a reputation for starting on time. In doing so, you will initiate a virtuous cycle whereby others will make sure they are on time for *your* meetings. In the early days, you may need to inform people in advance that your meeting will begin promptly. A more aggressive stance is to start your meetings on time no matter what without backtracking to recap for stragglers. That will send a clear message. Also, set up any presentations or handouts in advance.

Of the two sins, running over is the greater one. Chances are, participants have back to back meetings and you will be the one responsible for making them late for their next appointment. Needless to say, that is not an endearing quality. Moreover, when time is up, you can pretty much guarantee that you have lost people's attention. To end on time, you need to anticipate the likely arc and outcomes of the meeting. As a best practice, reserve at least five minutes at the end of a half hour meeting and at least ten minutes at the end of an hour long meeting to define next steps. Never, ever fall into the amateur trap of rushing a meeting at the end.

Inform participants of the meeting purpose, people, and process

The three "P's" of meetings that matter are purpose, process, and people. Among the three, process is the most important. You should make it a habit to start every meeting by identifying precisely what outcome you expect to achieve by the end. For example, you might state, "By the end of today's meeting, we will decide which new product to launch next quarter." Your mission is to give participants a clear and unambiguous picture of what success looks like so everyone can work together toward a common goal.

The second "P", process, establishes the structure of the meeting. Will the meeting format be brainstorming, discussion followed by questions and answers, or an interactive session? People that attend your meetings will appreciate being given a mental model for when and how to participate.

The final "P", people, is important but often abused. The key is to make sure that people know each other and understand why others are in the room. In smaller meetings of no more than five people, a quick round of introductions may be warranted. The abuse comes in larger meetings. I have no doubt that you have attended a meeting with ten or fifteen minutes wasted on round robin introductions. By the time the last person basks in their verbal resume, most people have already forgotten about everyone else not to mention the meeting objective. In this situation, you have two choices. If time permits, then get everyone together a few minutes early to conduct social niceties and exchange business cards. If time does not, then dive into the meeting. People's roles and responsibilities, as well as what they have to offer, will become rapidly clear.

Communicate progress and follow through on next steps

In truth, no one ever runs through the halls screaming, "Wow, Emma just ran an AWESOME meeting!!!" Instead, they gradually develop a subconscious awareness that "I respect Emma because she gets things done."

Follow through is the real measure of a manager that is great at running meetings that matter. At the end of every gathering, you should have captured and communicated a set of next steps. Ideally, these next steps should have well defined individual owners and objectives. After the meeting, it is your job to monitor open action items and report back to the group on progress and ultimate completion.

Recap

Here are the concepts you can immediately apply to become adept at running meetings that matter:
* Pre-syndicate your ideas with key players BEFORE you get to the meeting
* Start and end your meetings on time
* Inform participants of the meeting purpose, people, and process
* Communicate progress and follow through on next steps

PART TWO:

SALES, MARKETING,
AND
SERVICE

Chapter Nine: Customer Satisfaction and Loyalty

A war has been raging for decades over whether or not customer satisfaction and loyalty drive profitability. Proponents reasonably argue that happy customers will pay more, buy more, and spread goodwill through word of mouth. Similarly, every marketer has heard the warning that an unhappy customer will condemn you directly to ten of his or her friends. In the age of ubiquitous communications, an unhappy customer can indirectly trash you to billions of people. The position of the proponents requires little further illustration.

Skeptics of the link between customer satisfaction and profitability actually make a convincing case, too. The argument goes that there are tradeoffs between customer satisfaction and other factors that drive profitability – in particular, a tradeoff between productivity and satisfaction.

Take the business of delivering print newspapers. Imagine that a newspaper delivery service makes sure that customers get a paper delivered to their property in good condition by eight in the morning come rain or shine. This newspaper company could provide exceptional customer satisfaction by making sure that every paper is delivered with consistent daily precision on the mat at your front door. To guarantee that level of service, the newspaper company would have to hire a lot more delivery people since the productivity per employee would drop precipitously. Without raising prices, that extra cost would obliterate profits. Newspaper companies figured this out a long time ago. so your mornings, like mine, probably begin with an exciting treasure hunt through front yard hedges (assuming you don't get your news solely electronically).

Back in 1997, Eugene Anderson and Claes Fornell from the University of Michigan, along with Roland Rust of Vanderbilt University, published an extensive study on the relationship between productivity, customer satisfaction, and profitability. In 12 out of 16 industries they studied, businesses with high customer satisfaction measures earned higher average return on investment than those with low satisfaction. The four exceptions were department stores, gas stations, newspapers, and supermarkets. The characteristic these four shared relative to the other twelve was some degree of monopoly protection generally conferred by location advantage. In each of the four, people would clearly have a better experience if the companies in question added extra human capacity.

Though academics will split hairs for years to come, your common sense tells you that it pays to deliver great customer satisfaction. Great satisfaction is not meant to be blind and absolute. Rather your goal is to optimize customer satisfaction in a profit maximizing fashion. (Yes, there is that pesky efficient frontier concept again.)

You have no doubt noticed that I have been playing a bit fast and loose with the terms 'customer satisfaction' and 'customer loyalty'. Now, I will get a bit more precise. Of the two concepts, customer loyalty is the more powerful one, because customer satisfaction is merely an ingredient of customer loyalty. A satisfied customer may or may not come back for more. A satisfied customer may or may not tell his or her friends. A loyal customer will do both; he or she is a repeat satisfied customer who also spreads the good word about your product or service.

To build great loyalty, you need to measure it and continuously optimize it. Here is how to do that.

Measure customer loyalty

Fred Reichheld, a management consultant at Bain & Company, wrote the most compelling and most accessible book on customer loyalty, *The Ultimate Question: Driving Good Profits and True Growth*. While the following summary is no substitute for reading it cover to cover, I'll attempt to distill its key lessons.

More accurately, Mr. Reichheld's book should have been titled *The Ultimate Questions*, since he recommends a quality survey that has one question to measure loyalty and one question that allows you to continuously optimize it. Let us explore the measurement question first.

The ultimate loyalty measurement question is the following: "On a scale of 0 to 10, how likely is it that you would recommend [Company X] to a friend or colleague?" I have come across many brilliant and well-intentioned people that have embraced this question but missed one of the key subtleties: they apply a 1 to 5 scale to measure loyalty. Now, that can make for a good measurement. But, to be great, Reichheld prescribes a 0 to 10 scale.

Though this seems like nitpicking, the expanded scale is necessary to determine the Net Promoter Score (NPS) ™ for your product or service. The NPS is calculated by starting with the percentage of "Promoters", subtracting the percentage of "Detractors", and ignoring the "Passives." These three groups are defined as follows with respect to how they respond on the 0 to 10 scale:
- Promoters (response 9 or 10): These are the customers that really love you.
- Passives (response 7 or 8): These are the customers that are merely satisfied.
- Detractors: (response 0 to 6): These are the customers that hate you, but have varying degrees of kindness.

By way of example, imagine that you survey 500 people and get 30% promoters, 60% passives, and 10% detractors. Your resulting Net Promoter Score™ is 20% (computed as 30% minus 10%). The average firm tends to have scores between 5% and 10%, though negative scores are all too common.

In the absolute, the Net Promoter Score probably paints a rosier picture of customer loyalty than reality since the people that truly despise you will not do you the favor of responding to your survey. However, great loyalty managers focus primarily on the trend of their score over time and secondarily on their score relative to the competition.

Though the Net Promoter score has its own detractors, I challenge you to find a loyalty measurement that comes even close in simultaneously being easy to apply and easy to interpret. Start a continuous process today to measure customer loyalty that relies on this concept.

Optimize customer loyalty

In my opinion, the ultimate customer loyalty survey has not one but two questions (and preferably no more than two). Measuring loyalty alone will tell you how healthy you are at a given point in time. However, to figure out what you need to do to get a more steadfast following, you need to listen to your customers.

To optimize customer allegiance, you must ask the question: "What key improvement can we provide that would make you more likely to recommend us?" The wording here is flexible, but the gist is to ask a straightforward question that will elicit improvement ideas from your customers. From the promoters, you will learn why they came to love you in the first place and what you need to do to earn their continued loyalty. From the passives, you will learn the potentially modest steps you can take to transform them into promoters. And from the detractors, you just might figure out what it will take to convince them to stop posting nasty comments about your company all over the Internet.

As with any survey, your mission is to find the common threads and select the actions that deliver the greatest impact taking cost into account. While it is true that your customers will not necessarily suggest every valuable idea, they will suggest most of them, and rest assured that the ones they suggest do matter.

If you ask people what they want, then you need to be prepared to systematically address their requests. At the very least, you must acknowledge desires and provide an informational reply. In many instances, customers will cite immediate product or service failures that need to be addressed. Research shows that customers who complained and had their problems solved are significantly more loyal as a group than customers that never had a known problem to begin with. However, if a customer highlights a problem and you do nothing, then you can pretty much write them off. It might have been better never to have asked in the first place.

Recap

In almost all industries, customer loyalty drives profitable growth. To become a great loyalty manager, you must institute an ongoing program to:
- Measure customer loyalty
- Optimize customer loyalty

Chapter Ten: Selling to Executives

You would think that every professional services firm on the planet would be well versed in consultative sales practices. And yet, I am sure you have had a recent experience with a potential supplier who spent the first forty minutes of a one hour initial meeting walking you through a set of slides detailing his or her background, capabilities, and so on. If you are lucky, the presenter started to ask you about your needs with the little time left at the end. On paper, this is a glaringly terrible practice. And yet, these meetings happen thousands of times every day.

The wonderful news is that the pervasiveness of bad sales behavior creates a golden opportunity for you. To become proficient at selling to executives, you need to adopt a few simple practices.

First identify the value

The days of most executives are filled with back-to-back constructive problem solving meetings where they are asked to make thoughtful, albeit rapid, decisions. When presenting to an executive, the best internal staff lay out the facts, discuss problems or opportunities, and bring forth potential solutions. Since this is the language that executives speak, you should be fluent when engaging them on your products and services.

Selling the value means working with the executive to construct a forward looking plan that will deliver tangible results to their entire business. To do that, you need to ask questions, listen, and be diagnostic. By understanding your customers' strategies and their critical problems, you become a consultative partner in the best position to link the unique benefits of your solutions to their needs.

Selling the value does not mean describing your features, functionality, and capabilities. Most executives have no time and no interest in that level of detail.

To be great at selling to executives, imagine that your job is to make them a hero to their company. Executives become heroes by pulling strategic levers such as:

- increasing revenues
- lowering costs
- improving operational efficiency
- enhancing employee productivity

Once you have uncovered the executive's strategies and problems and linked the unique benefits of your service to clear bottom line business results, you have another key responsibility. Good sales people work hard to understand what it will take to commit to buying. Great sales people also work to understand why the customer will not buy and then work systematically to overcome objections.

Establish yourself as a trusted partner

At some point, a prospect will narrow their purchasing decision down to you and to one or two of your closest competitors. You can safely assume that the prospect has a sense of near equivalence between your company and the alternative suppliers when product attributes, service, pricing, and so on are netted out. In the end, their decision will come down to which supplier he or she puts the most trust in to deliver on the promised value.

To get over the risk of buying your product or service, you must prove how you help clients to be consistently successful over the long term. The most effective ways to offer proof are by providing references or by sharing case studies that are directly relevant. Moreover, since you are selling to human beings, you should address not only the business value delivered, but also the individual personal value realized.

The consultative approach that you take during the sales process builds trust. By listening and bringing new ideas, rather than purely pitching your wares, you establish that you care about the client and his or her barriers to business and personal success.

Finally, to build trust, you must demonstrate that you are always prepared. This begins in the very first meeting that you have with your prospects. Prior to that meeting, you must do your homework on their company and their individual goals so that you are fully primed to discuss their business. Preparation should continue to remain supreme in every subsequent interaction so the client has the security that they can depend on you.

Determine the customer's purchasing process

Successful sales people know that one of the most critical tasks is figuring out who holds the purse strings in the organization. In recent years, mid level managers have lost purchasing authority, though they do not care to readily admit it.

An excellent strategy to completely determine the key decision maker is to ask the prospect who in the organization will be involved in the purchasing process. This allows the prospect to save face. In the process, you will learn if the person's manager, manager's manager, CFO, or even CEO needs to be brought in. When they identify these people, you gain the ability to architect ongoing access to power. You are within your right to require one-on-one interviews or a kick off meeting with all stakeholders early on. Moreover, you are within your right to require periodic status meetings with the key participants.

Develop a written value plan with your client
during the sales process

While it is possible to shepherd a complex sale from early consultation to proposal without a formal roadmap, there is a better way. Early in the process, skillful sales executives create a written value plan in partnership with the prospect. This plan should cover every stage of the sales cycle including pre-sale, purchase order to go live, and go live to value realization. Depending on the situation, it can be as informal as an email or as formal as a prepared document.

For starters, this plan gives your prospect that confidence that you are in it for the long haul and not just for your commission check. It proves that you understand the outcome is business and personal value realization and not a signed purchase order.

Most importantly, the value plan is also an excellent place for you to capture and address client objections. Ultimately, you want the document to build commitment that the prospect will purchase, provided you meet clearly articulated criteria.

Manage the change process for the customer

Once you have a signed deal, your work is only just beginning. In years past, you would simply ship your product to the customer with an instruction manual and be done with it. That worked reasonably well in the age of relatively unsophisticated products and less demanding customers. Today, you should take on the responsibility of managing the customer through the change process required to get the expected return on investment from your product.

By way of example, a plethora of studies have examined the percentage of customer relationship management (CRM) software installations that succeed and that fail. It turns out that approximately 20% of all CRM projects completely fail to deploy and another 50% do not provide meaningful return on investment. Given that the CRM market as of this writing is about $10 billion, companies are collectively pouring $7 billion down the drain. And, that $7 billion does not include untold billions in additional services, wasted time, and opportunity cost.

The big problem with CRM projects, and more generally with projects involving sophisticated products and services, is that suppliers rely on their customers to enact the change required for success. Inevitably, however, customers systematically underestimate the degree of change required and lack direct experience in getting value from your offering.

As the supplier, you have the most knowledge and experience of what it takes for customers to get value from your product. You will have seen the change processes that deliver success and those that result in failure. You have a moral and professional responsibility to manage the change processes on behalf of your customer.

Conduct Regular Value Reviews

I am willing to bet that most of your suppliers disappear after the sale and only magically reappear a month or two before you are expected to make your next purchase. I am also willing to bet that you find that unsavory.

Fortunately, there is a higher ground that you can reach which will make you stellar at selling to executives. That higher ground is reached by conducting periodic value reviews with your customer. During a value review, you have two main objectives.

The first objective is to collect and communicate feedback. If you did your job well during the initial sale, then the executive has a tangible set of expectations of the value that you will deliver. Ask the scary questions. Did we deliver what we promised? What could we have done differently? Also, gather insights on what went especially well. In many cases, the executive will not have direct knowledge of value received. Therefore, the opportunity rests with you to amass and communicate information from your people and systems and, more critically, from other individuals inside the executive's company. Statements confirming value that are made by individuals in the executive's own company are a thousand times more powerful than your own data or estimates.

During the value review, your second objective is to optimize value after the sale. This is your opportunity to suggest additional best practices and applications for your product or service. In short, it is your opportunity to delight your customer with service in a way that transforms you from just another sales person into a trusted partner.

At the end of the contract period, you should be able to confirm effortlessly that you met or exceeded the value the executive expected. By capturing feedback along the way, you avoid the scramble of trying to piece together the long forgotten past.

Create a new value plan to extend your relationship

During the course of periodic value reviews, you will have picked up on many opportunities to deliver new solutions in the next sales cycle. At the end of the contract period, go back into consultative selling mode. Take the time to uncover new unsolved problems as well as the executive's updated strategic priorities. With that information, you can create a new value plan to extend your relationship.

Recap

Odds are that your competitors are lousy at consultative selling. You can excel by establishing value, ensuring that it gets delivered, and confirming the success of your relationship. Here are the concepts you can immediately apply to become great at selling to executives:

- First identify the value
- Establish yourself as a trusted partner
- Determine the customer's purchasing process
- Develop a written value plan with your client during the sales process
- Manage the change process for the customer
- Conduct Regular Value Reviews
- Create a new value plan to extend your relationship

Chapter Eleven:
Messaging Effectiveness

Exceptional managers need to possess superb writing skills whether they are drafting presentations or banging out e-mails. Under time pressure, it is all too easy to let the effectiveness of your messaging slip. To combat mediocrity, you should impose the 'plan then write then edit' discipline in all of your communications. Variously attributed to Mark Twain, Blaise Pascal, Marcus Tullius Cicero, and a host of other scribes and scholars, the hoary "If I had more time, I would have written you a shorter letter" is still one of my favorite quotes. Take that advice to heart during the planning and editing phases.

Plan

At some point in our writing lives, we are all told to plan. The prescription, more often than not, is structural, rather than conceptual. More concretely, a teacher coaches us to create an outline with an introduction, three main points, and a conclusion. Sound advice, to be sure; but you can up the ante.

The first step in planning to write copy that captures is selecting your audience. Whether you are writing to a large audience or a single person, picture a single individual in your mind's eye. By way of example, imagine that you are marketing pediatric dental services. Rather than thinking abstractly about parents, develop a vivid image of a mother with two young children. Build out a persona including her name, her age, her likes, her dislikes.

After conjuring your muse, the next step in planning is to determine the benefits that are important to your audience. Keeping their needs front and center will help you stay focused on their ego not yours. For example, the mother that you have called to mind probably does not care about features of your practice such as the number of square feet, your panoramic digital x-ray machine, or your brand of tooth polish. Instead, you should focus on how your practice serves the physical (hygiene, limited radiation, allergy awareness) and emotional (empathy, entertainment) needs of children and their families.

The last step, often the hardest to commit to in the planning process, is to state one – just one – specific objective that you are trying to achieve in your writing. Though you will be tempted to extol every virtue, remember that less is more.

Write

Once you have identified your audience and chosen a single objective, it is time to start writing. Let go of perfection and just write. Allow the words to flow. Whatever you do, absolutely, positively, DO NOT EDIT YET; that will come later.

As you write, adopt a conversational tone and let your personality come through. In the planning phase, you conjured the image of a specific person. Imagining that you are having a dialogue with this individual puts that task of drafting on a human scale, allowing you to create messages that are directly relevant on a personal level. A practice that some great copy writers employ is not only to imagine a particular person, but also to pretend the individual is a loved one to whom they are writing a personal letter.

In the course of committing words to paper, frequently you are going to get a nagging feeling that something you have written will elicit a question from the imagined conversation partner. Pay close attention to that inner voice. Those questions might probe for additional clarification or they may be outright objections. You should anticipate and answer questions as your muse would raise them.

As you become a more seasoned writer, you should engender curiosity. There are two smart ways to do this. The first is to introduce ideas that challenge conventional wisdom. Specifically, with respect to the individual you have conjured, provide information that subtly confronts that person's belief system. After all, there is a reason that conservatives spend a lot of time consuming liberal media and vice versa. The second approach to manufacturing interest is to create a knowledge gap or surprise that makes your audience ask 'how?' or 'why?'

The language and the style you employ are both critical. Write short sentences with simple active words. Use clear language. Employ repetition. Instead of "Eradicate inane matters to culminate in increased work productivity", try "remove waste to drive results."

Since you took the time in the planning stage to develop a persona of a distinct individual, you should now use language that paints a vivid mental picture or story for him or her. After all, you are writing to inspire curiosity. To do that, draw upon words that evoke positive emotions and stimulate the senses. Examples include: wonder, imagine, reveal, story, discover, rivet, inspire, and picture

As a writer, one of your aims is to ensure that your audience trusts your message. To make your message credible, call upon external sources for proof when possible. For example, I could simply tell you that children experience less anxiety if they observe their mothers being treated by a dental hygienist before having their own teeth cleaned. It is far more powerful for me to cite an international study published in the Journal of Canadian Dentistry. Consider a a May 2009 study of 155 children bythe head of the department of pediatric and community dentistry at Saint Joseph University and the head of a pediatric dental clinic. The researchers found that children who first see procedures modeled on their mothers have an average heart rate of 96 beats per minute versus 102 beats per minute when modeled on fathers or when not modeled at all. Sorry dads.

Edit

Once you have completed your first draft, reward yourself by taking a break. Fierce editing demands a clear mind. While the goal in the writing process is to unleash ideas, the goal in the editing process principally is to polish language and secondarily to fill in the occasional gap.

In your first edit, focus on the overarching objective that you defined in the planning phase. As you encounter any text that does not serve your singular goal, ruthlessly delete, no matter how hard it is.

In your second edit, strive to make the language even more clear, riveting, and sensory. Break long sentences into shorter ones. Transform passive tense into active tense. Eliminate jargon and highfalutin words.

In your third edit, put yourself in the mind of your reader. Raise objections when you see flaws in logic or ask for clarification when you are confused. During this revision, you may want to engage the services of a friend or co-worker to play the role of the audience. Over time, you may develop a knack for doing this on your own, but there is never shame in drawing upon another pair of eyes.

Depending on how much time you have and how important the copy you are writing, you can go through the three edits in successive waves.

My final piece of advice is to finish what you start as well as you can and then release your writing into the world. You do the best you can with the time you have. Completion, not perfection, is the goal. Even Twain and Cicero knew that, at some point, they had to let go and just send their letters.

Recap

Here are the concepts you can immediately apply to write copy that captures:
- Plan
- Write
- Edit

Chapter Twelve:
Product Management

In most organizations, the critical skill for a successful product manager is best summed up as influence at a distance. Whether the product management function reports in to sales, marketing, or a standalone business unit, there are a distinct set of best practices your team can follow to be successful.

Architect and optimize the channel

If account executives are not selling your product, then you and your team are not going to be around for very long. A fortunate few may have a dedicated sales force with total focus on your product. Most product managers, however, need to compete with other project managers for the attention of sales people. The formula becomes the following: you sell to your sales team and they sell to your customers.

First and foremost, you must keep your messaging simple. Salespeople, just like all other people on the planet, are bombarded with messages. Though your product may have fifty incredible features, you want to arm your sales force with just two things. First, you should train them on the fundamental value proposition of the product. When sales people are in a meeting and a prospect articulates a problem that your product uniquely addresses, you want a spotlight to shine on your offering in the account executive's mind. Second, you should ensure that the sales person has an unambiguous understanding of what is in it for him or her personally if he sells your product. Though many rewards are financial, never underestimate the power of recognition – especially public recognition among one's peers.

With only one of you and a great many salespeople, you need to be strategic about where you direct your effort. Some product managers focus on broadcast messages to the entire sales force. Others target the head of sales hoping for messages to work their way down. Both of these approaches are suboptimal and the reason has everything to do with basic organizational behavior. The bottom line is that people do what their managers expect of them. Just think of yourself, for instance, sitting in a large, all company meeting where you CEO lays out her high level vision for the next year. If your boss does not set objectives and manage daily expectations to that vision, then you and your colleagues are unlikely to react. Taking this message to heart, you will have the most impact as a product manager if you concentrate your effort on first line sales managers.

I can hear your objection already – "but, there are too many of them!" To avoid this pickle, you simply need to recognize another key organizational behavior principle. Human beings, yes that includes sales managers, move as a herd. Even in a herd, a few brave souls wander into uncharted territory looking for sustenance. In the early stages, these people will appear as widely distributed bright spots. As you identify them, interview them to learn their best practices and lessons learned and systematically promote those findings to other managers. As you help these teams win business, they will virally communicate their success. Ultimately, products perform best when sales people can ask other sales people for advice. When that happens, you have prevailed.

Know your end customer

If you market exclusively to your sales force, then you will rapidly lose touch with the changing needs of your customers. Perhaps more importantly, you may fail to capture innovative, unconventional uses for your product. Just think of Arm and Hammer baking soda, which is no more than run of the mill sodium bicarbonate in a box. By experimenting internally and by listening to customers, their product has found its way into laundry detergent, toothpaste, swimming pool cleaning tablets, carpet deodorizer, and many other uses.

The easiest way to keep in touch with what your customers care about is to involve yourself in specific deals. Though you will need to establish trust, most sales people will willingly pull you in as an expert to help them close business.

A more powerful approach for staying in touch with the needs of the market is to create a continual feedback loop. Quantitative surveys are a necessary but insufficient approach. You should also have a regular cadence of live, qualitative interviews. Most critically, this is not something that you can delegate; be there to listen and to ask probing questions.

Prioritize innovation

During the course of the conversations that you have with new and prospective clients, with sales people, and with other interested parties, you will have your hands full with a laundry list of innovations. Since time and money are limited, you must prioritize those items that will have the greatest impact on your business.

Hence, as a product manager, you should focus on big, hairy projects. (Unfortunately, this also means that you will likely end up de-emphasizing maintenance.) As you place bets on a limited set of initiatives, you should monitor in an unbiased way so that you can reprioritize, iterate, and occasionally terminate. Take the time to choose projects that are likely to succeed and marshal every available resource. You want to become known as someone that achieves results, not someone that is constantly tinkering and changing direction.

Introduce change gradually

Everybody likes to have a clean slate. Consequently, most people craft plans to roll out change on a massive scale. However, the most effective product managers introduce change gradually. Whenever you would like to make a modification, ask yourself how you can run a pilot. This test will not only provide you with fact-based evidence that the change will work, but also give you guidance on ways to improve how and what you roll out. In addition to dedication to using pilot programs, you should also seek to break change into multiple phases, each providing the ability to communicate unambiguous short term wins.

Recap

Here are the concepts you can immediately apply to become a great product manager:
- Architect and optimize the channel
- Know your customer
- Prioritize innovation
- Introduce change gradually

Chapter Thirteen: Webinars

These days, no self-respecting lead generation engine is complete without a web-based seminar program. Live and even recorded Webinars are a low cost way to find and pre-qualify prospective customers. These sessions are particularly effective for professional, knowledge based services which have a high cost of direct sales.

Drive registration

Just like every marketing program, the beginning of the Webinar funnel begins with getting behinds in seats. Here, of course, content is king. You must select content that aligns the interests of the target audience with the specific benefits your product provides. Remember that people attend Webinars to learn, not to be sold something.

The title that you create will have an amazing impact on the registration rate. Craft a title that clearly tells the audience what is in it for them; edit it mercilessly to ensure that you accomplish this in as few words as possible.

In some circumstances, it may make sense to build a Webinar community as part of a larger social networking experience. If you go this route, then you can develop a series of Webinars adhering to a theme. However, tread cautiously here. The ultimate goal of Webinar programs is to accelerate the sales cycle. By deploying a sequence, prospects may feel compelled to wait until the end of the series to pass judgment on the value of your solution.

Every additional field of information that you request on the registration page will lower the registration rate. To that end, simplify the registration page to the bare bones. Asking for email addresses alone will provide the maximum number of leads. However, you will probably need to have enough information to route leads to specific sales territories based on vertical market, geography, or named account. In that case, you can ask for an email address and phone number. By linking the email domain to a company name and the area code to geography, you will have everything that you need. Moreover, asking for a phone number will serve to filter out less qualified parties. To make sure that your Webinar really hits the mark, optionally you can solicit advance questions on the confirmation page.

Since it may require multiple touches to entice people to register for your Webinar, a typical best practice is to begin promoting the event twenty-one days in advance. Though you can start as much as a month in advance, people generally will not respond to a solicitation for something that is more than thirty days away. In terms of scheduling, Wednesdays and Thursdays between 11 am and 1pm are the optimal times. If you have filled the calendar for those days, then Tuesdays are the next best choice. You should avoid Mondays and Fridays, since those days are unlikely to provide an acceptable return on investment.

Drive attendance

Getting people to register for your Webinar is only the first part of the battle. The next hurdle is actually getting them to show up. You should expect registration-to-attendance ratios to range from 25% for general interest topics to 50% for specialized topics with a highly targeted audience. Of course, if you have exceptionally valuable content and people who actually paid to attend, then attendance rates can be as high as 90%.

The first way to increase attendance rates is to make remembering to attend the Webinar as effortless as possible. At minimum, you should send a registration confirmation that includes an electronic calendar attachment. In addition, industry best practice dictates sending a reminder one day before as well as one to three hours in advance of the session.

A second compelling way to drive attendance is to offer a reward. One form of this is offering a monetary or otherwise fashionable prize to randomly selected attendees. However, you can do better, particularly if you are focused on a specialized topic. For example, if you are a customer relationship management software vendor extolling the virtues of using technology to improve client relationships, then you could offer an exclusive and directly relevant whitepaper or electronic book to all attendees.

Deliver content

Congratulations, you not only got people to register for your Webinar, but also enticed them to hear what you have to say. But, since attention spans are short and Webinars rely on influence at a distance, you have your work cut out for you.

A first best practice is to load the most valuable content at the front end. This will serve to engage your audience. In addition, you will demonstrate that the session has value even for those that drop early.

A second best practice is to manage your speaking tone. As you would with a live audience, speak with passion and enthusiasm, almost as if you are speaking with one individual rather than broadcasting to a group.

A third best practice is to make the experience interactive. For example, you can integrate polling and discuss results as they are dynamically updated. Additionally, you may choose to integrate social media feeds into part of the display.

Though compelling Webinars are designed first and foremost to inform the audience, attendees know that your motivation for teaching them is not purely altruistic (unless you are doing a public service session). Hence, the webinar should end with a call to action that compels the attendees to escalate their involvement. For instance, consider soliciting them to fill out a post event survey in order to download a free copy of the presentation.

Drive and measure results

Webinars are a marketing activity designed to initiate or accelerate a sales cycle. Hence, registration rates and attendance rates are not in and of themselves adequate measures of success. To truly get a sense of any gains, then, monitor the return on investment by factoring revenues from converted clients against program costs. If you discover the program is not driving profits, then you can adjust it or shut it down and used the money for something with higher proven impact.

To maximize conversion rates, sales executives (or sales automation if you do not have a direct sales force) should respond immediately to attendees. In addition, it often pays to reach out to the fifty to seventy five percent of registrants that did not attend. For this latter group in particular, you may want to send an automatic invitation to your next Webinar.

Recap

Here are the concepts you can immediately apply to create a compelling Webinar program that delivers a high return on marketing investment:

- Drive registration
- Drive attendance
- Deliver content
- Drive and measure results

Chapter Fourteen:
Building Digital Communities

If you are seeking to develop deeper relationships with clients and prospects, then you will benefit from fostering a digital community. Conceptually, this is not new, as forward thinking companies have maintained high touch client advisory councils for years. What is new is that a digital community ups the game on both your ability to influence clients as well as your responsibility to learn from and react to user needs. Moreover, digital communities foster mass collaboration with participants, providing everything from ideas to functional products.

Recruit Community Members

First and foremost, people will be drawn to your digital community if you establish a concrete, shared value proposition. Moreover, the value proposition should provide a compelling need not met elsewhere. The most successful and compelling communities allow members to share information, best practices, and lessons learned in very specific domains. In a few instances, including the open source software movement, value is created by allowing participants to offer premium extensions and services. The breadth of a community like the online encyclopedia Wikipedia is more the exception than the rule. Some interesting communities with a targeted focus include Khan Academy and PerlMonks.

At Khan Academy, founder and executive director Salman Khan personally created a library of over 1,600 videos targeted at kindergarten through twelfth grade students struggling with math and science. Many of the concepts that Mr. Khan tackled were first requested by friends and family and later by a broader community. As of this writing, the Khan Academy model exemplifies a digital community with member solicited but centrally created content.

PerlMonks is a very different, and in some ways more traditional, digital community. The model in this instance is a loosely moderated discussion tread for people looking to polish their Perl (a software language) programming skills. The PerlMonks folks do a lot of clever things to nurture their community including live chat, tutorials, and yes, even Perl poetry. Super nerds that they are, the moderators explicitly state that verse can include poetry written in Perl, poetry generated by Perl scripts, and conventional poetry about Perl or PerlMonks. If you do not think the haiku "Cat please go away! Demanding my attention — does not help me code!" posted by "kitty love" is funny, then PerlMonks is not for you.

Building out a digital community, only to then wait for devotees is a sure road to disappointment. Start offline to be successful online. In the early phases, begin with a small, in-person advisory group of core enthusiasts. They will test and upgrade your value proposition and tell you what would make it worth their time to participate. This group should also take responsibility for crafting and maintaining a membership guide. Needless to say, the best enthusiasts are trusted influencers that bring their own large networks.

The live advisory board is one of several ways to confer a select status. Consider extending this feeling to the larger community by making membership in the group exclusive. The volunteers that run PerlMonks have elevated this to an art form. When a new user joins the forum, they enter the Monastery gates in probationary mode with few privileges. I once posted a question with incorrectly formatted computer code and received a thorough lashing in the form of a demotion. As people participate by asking and answering questions and by voting, they gain experience points. Over the course of time, an individual can move from Acolyte to Friar to Abbot and so on. In fact, there are twenty eight levels, culminating in Pope. In contrast to the real world, PerlMonks has three Popes as of this writing, one of whom is creator Tim Vroom.

Though the two communities profiled here have a not-for-profit educational mission, you can assemble digital communities around a for-profit product or service that rests on the same principles of sharing information, best practices, and lessons learned. When you allow your sales and marketing channel into the community, do so sparingly and make sure that any offers provide real value to members.

A final consideration around setting up a digital community is commitment. In the same way that people are wary of forming deep relationships, potential community members will be able to immediately smell whether you are in it for the long term. To demonstrate your commitment, you should provide adequate resources to build and sustain the community. At minimum, that means making a community the full time job of at least one (and preferably more) extroverted, digitally literate person.

Cultivate Community Members

If seeded properly with a concrete value proposition, a core set of influencers, and adequate infrastructure, your digital community will be off to a strong start. As the group evolves, you will need to review and enhance the value that members receive. You can approach this in the same way that you approach product development -- by exploring complementary needs of participants.

In the for-profit world, such enhancements are more likely to be sourced in offline meetings rather than online interactions. You can gain intimacy and build trust from quarterly face-to-face forums with your advisory council and other engaged members.

Create a community operating model

To thrive, digital communities not only need basic care and feeding, but also need an operating framework that is adaptive. People, of course, are at the heart of the model. The advisory group, or a complementary set of trusted partici-pants, bear the responsibility for guiding the community. In addition, this core group should be expected to handle exceptions to processes.

If you have ever read an un-moderated discussion thread in a public online forum, then you have seen some of the lowest forms of human behavior. Con-sequently, I strongly recommend building, at inception, mechanisms for quality control into your community. Appropriate techniques range from automated tools to remove content with objectionable language, to a fully moderated envi-ronment where information must be verified before sharing.

Communities that are expected to persist need to be self-replenishing to make up for participants that drop out. Choosing a distinct focus and serving a need not met elsewhere will go a long way to helping individuals self-select into the group. The key is to get the community large enough to benefit from positive network effects where an ever growing community is continuously adding more value.

Regardless of community size, strive to remain in constant communication with the group. This is especially important for smaller communities. Remember that communication can span across a range of engagement levels from e-mail to teleconferences to physical events.

Last but not least, build flexibility into the community infrastructure from the start. This means that systems should be modular, reconfigurable, and editable. With this capability, the core group of community leaders will be able to react rapidly to changing requirements.

Deliver Value

It is possible to create communities where some degree of value is delivered in tangible economic form. A common approach here is to create friendly competition with real prizes. If you do award prizes, then it is best to make them relevant to your product - think branded merchandise rather than cold hard cash. A minor problem with competition is that you create some losers along the way. However, the peskier drawbackwith tangible rewards is that they create the unwelcome aura of pay-to-play. A bad practice in any era, it is especially dangerous in an age when reputation – especially digital reputation – is an infinitely valued asset.

Of course, intangible value is far more powerful and ethically safe; thus, it should be the focus of your efforts. The PerlMonks experience system provides an excellent example that plays to social and emotional needs for status and recognition.

Recap

Here are the concepts you can immediately apply to become great at building digital communities:

- Recruit Community Members
- Cultivate Community Members
- Create a community operating model
- Deliver Value

Chapter Fifteen: Sales Force Effectiveness

There is a tremendous volume of literature on how to be a great individual sales person from the minds of gurus like Zig Zigler and Jeffrey Gitomer. However, wisdom on how to architect an effective group of salespeople is harder to come by. If you are in a position to reengineer sales strategy, the good news is that there are only a few critical levers you must consider.

The strategic levers include hiring, compensation, span of control, and territory assignment. The tactical levers include training and activity management. The strategic levers are the primary ones on which to concentrate. If those are set correctly, then account executives can overcome inadequate training and maintain a high level of activity.

Hire the right number of sales people with the right profile

One of the first principles of sales is to match your sales capacity to your production capacity. In most low fixed cost, high variable cost businesses like professional services, it is pretty easy to get this right. In contrast, for high fixed cost, low variable cost businesses like software or information services, enterprises often have the opportunity to double or even triple their sales force. After all, if you are not able to knock on the door to begin with, it is pretty unlikely you are going to sell anything.

Individual hiring managers should have a crystal clear understanding of what great looks like. In some environments, raw skills like clock speed, enthusiasm, and assertiveness may be required. In others, you may be willing to sacrifice some raw sales ability for industry specific knowledge. To figure out the right hiring profile, find the common threads in the background and skills of your current top performers. You will have to compare the top performers to the bottom performers to identify the critical differences that drive success. When you single out the top and bottom performers, use long term, fact-based results and not just managers' opinions.

Align compensation with overall strategic objectives

Total sales compensation is a blend of base salary, commission, and special incentives. Each of these should be tuned to align with overall strategic objectives. Specifically, develop a solid understanding of how the compensation system will affect individual sales professionals as well as overall profitability.

The chosen split between base salary and commission is highly dependent on your environment. For example, if your organization has fixed production capacity that you expect to sell out, then the most appropriate structure is one with a high base salary and low commission. However, sales professionals are universally motivated by the compensation upside promised by a high commission rate. Unfortunately, an extreme structure – such as one with straight commission - will generally draw less experienced, more aggressive, and potentially less loyal people into your organization. The key is to strike a balance factoring in the expected behaviors and the implied skill profile that your system will elicit.

The simplest structure is to pay a flat commission rate on all sales beyond an established quota. Note that the quota can be zero. Since you get what you pay for, you can then add complexity to the compensation structure. For example, you might want to set higher rates on products that are known to drive better client retention rates and expanded purchasing of complementary offerings. Alternatively, you may wish to establish a tiered commission structure where rates increase with sales volume in order to dangle an ever more delicious carrot in front of star performers. As you make such adjustments, tread very carefully; the hallmark of a great compensation structure is simplicity. As a rule of thumb, you should be confident that the typical sales person can determine his or her payout from the next sale on the fly, without so much as resorting to a calculator. If the sales person needs to look up a table or a spreadsheet, then you need to go back to the drawing board.

If you operate in the nearly fictional world where you have fixed capacity, your product cannot be inventoried, and clients refuse to wait for delivery, then you can set a cap on total compensation to prevent dissatisfied customers. For everyone else, never set a cap on compensation even if that means your best sales person earns more than your CEO. Paying sales commissions is like paying taxes. If you pay a large amount of taxes or commissions, then that is the kind of problem you want to have.

Optimize the span of control

Span of control is a term with military origins that simply means the number of professionals that directly report to a first line manager. An excessively low span of control is both expensive and has adverse effects on sales effectiveness since it brings de-motivating micromanagement. In contrast, an overly high span of control also lowers productivity. In such an environment, managers are left with little time to provide coaching and critical deal support.

Sales managers split their time between administrative tasks, planning, and coaching. Administrative tasks include forecasting, responding to corporate requests and communications, and managing human resources issues. Planning includes such functions as account strategy and analysis as well as personal career development. Coaching includes time spent one on one with sales executives and time spent with your team on their visits in the field. Each of these three major categories consumes roughly a third of a sales manager's time. Hence, a forty hour work week includes just thirteen hours that a manager can spend with a direct report.

In a low complexity, high volume environment such as retail sales or a call center, the span of control can equal or exceed fifteen direct reports to one manager since the need for coaching and for exception handling is minimal. However, in typical environments a span of control ranging from four-to-one to eight-to-one is considered optimal as that allows the manager one to three hours per week to support each team member.

Match territory assignment to required knowledge

When most people think of sales strategy, they think of how individual sales people are assigned to their own personal pumpkin patch. Though the word territory implies geographic segmentation, an assignment formula can be a mix of geography, industry, client role, product, or other factors.

The right territory strategy depends primarily on the knowledge base that sales people must possess to effectively close business. The more that client needs are governed by job role or industry, the more narrowly you will need to define territories. Generally, you can expect the typical sales person to be able to go deep in only one industry or one highly complex product. A more focused territory definition allows account executives to build a critical mass of knowledge allowing them to be successful with a consultative selling approach. On the other extreme, if you offer a low complexity product with broad appeal, then you can get away with pure geographic territory assignment.

Provide adequate sales training

Though formal sales training has its value, you can count on your account executives to learn on the job both through self study and from peers, provided they have a motivating compensation structure and a fertile territory. That said, it would be folly to dismiss formal training outright.

Since most sales people are extroverted experiential learners, the most effective approach to skill building is role playing exercises that come as close as possible to the real world they will encounter. These simulated live fire situations should be staged in a group setting. Raising the stakes through social pressure will make the account executive less likely to choke in an actual client engagement. Additionally, even those observing will gain a tremendous amount of value. A distant though still acceptable alternative is electronic (strictly video) learning modules that include questions to test and cement knowledge. You can safely assume that any reading material will at best find its way quickly into the recycling bin.

The key focus areas for training include order processing, basic selling skills, and product knowledge. Every sales person will require training on the mechanics of order processing. The less experienced your sales force, the more emphasis you will need to place on basic selling skills. Similarly, the more complex your product, the more time you will need to spend training account executives on features. However, be aware of the following key danger. With an extremely complex product, sales people fall into the trap of engaging prospective clients in discussions about features and functionality, thus wasting valuable time that could be spent on value-based selling, instead. After all, they spent hours mastering this knowledge themselves. To combat this, maintain a constant emphasis on consultative, value-based selling techniques and make it clear that feature selling is not acceptable.

Though order processing, selling skills and product knowledge are fertile ground for formal training, industry instruction is conspicuously absent. If industry expertise is a critical factor in winning business, then it is worth hiring professionals that come from the prospective companies to which you are selling. Thriving sales executives will enhance their vertical market knowledge on an ongoing basis through client and prospect interactions and by browsing offline and online periodicals.

Encourage activity that drives results

Like sales training, activity management is a tactical lever that you can worry less about if you have properly tuned the strategic levers of hiring, compensation, span of control, and territory assignment. When it comes to time management for sales executives, you should first explore if you are your own worst enemy. Are your account executives being dragged down by excessive internal meetings? Are you slamming them with administrative overhead that can be eliminated or redirected to a centralized team? Are you filling their inboxes with excessive and unfocused internal communications? Clearing this clutter may be all you need to do to drive a huge increase in sales effectiveness.

If you need a little extra juice, then you can set an achievable expectation for the volume of sales activity per week. This is particularly effective for less experienced sales people and in high transaction volume environments. Remember that this is a fairly aggressive tactic that also consumes cycles since sales people must enter activity into a tracking system. Micro-managing sales activity should be used sparingly since it tacitly communicates a lower level of trust and limits perceived independence. If you do go down this path for sales people tasked with both renewing existing business and growing new business, then you may need to be prescriptive about the split between these two activities. To make such expectations have an impact, sales people must know that the information is being monitored and is tied to rewards or consequences.

Recap

Here are the concepts you can immediately apply to become an adroit manager of sales effectiveness:

- Hire the right number of sales people with the right profile
- Align compensation with overall strategic objectives
- Optimize the span of control
- Match territory assignment required knowledge
- Provide adequate sales training
- Encourage activity that drives results

PART THREE:

STRATEGY
AND
PLANNING

Chapter Sixteen: Negotiation

The first step to becoming a deft negotiator is realizing that everything can be negotiated. In many situations, such as employment agreements and home purchases, virtually everyone knows that they can and should negotiate the price. In other transactions, including buying clothing at a department store or booking a hotel room, most people are conditioned to accept the formally printed sticker price without batting an eyelash.

In general, people expect the price to be negotiable on expensive transactions, but accept the price on inexpensive ones. This phenomenon is rooted in two considerations, one valid and one not.

The first consideration, perfectly valid, is that there is a tradeoff between negotiation and time. Though it would not make sense to negotiate for a week to get a twenty percent discount on a $50 item of clothing, it does make sense to spend the time if you are buying a $500,000 home.

The second, unfounded, consideration is rooted in the ubiquitous human behavior of conflict avoidance. Many people require a minimum amount of expected benefit before they will even begin to negotiate. This minimum amount is required to compensate them for the stress of engaging in perceived conflict. If you view every opportunity to negotiate as a pleasurable learning experience, then the threshold quickly drops to zero. In fact, people invest good time and money to enter such conflict when they take a negotiation class.

Putting the factors of the very real time tradeoff and the unjustified conflict fear together, you can see that it makes sense at least to try to negotiate for that $50 piece of clothing. If you expect to get $50 or more of value out it, then the worst that can happen is that the sales clerk will not budge on the price. It is worth thirty seconds to figure this out no matter how wealthy you are.

Keen negotiators also know that price is not the only attribute in the mix. You can negotiate most elements of a transaction, including timing, quantity, quality, and additional services. You should concentrate on the manageable set of factors that matter to you and to the party with whom you are negotiating.

Though everything can be negotiated, it does not mean that everything should be. If you do negotiate literally everything, you friends will desert you and your significant other will leave you. As in all things, find the balance.

The following tips, with practice, rapidly will turn you into an incisive negotiator.

Gain an information advantage before you start negotiating

The single greatest factor that separates good (and sadly poor) negotiators from great ones is the effort spent gaining an information advantage before the formal negotiation even begins. Within your given time constraints, your mission is to gather as much intelligence on both tangible and intangible data.

Imagine that you have found a home that you want to purchase. Most people begin their quest by researching tangible data. For example, at what price have comparable properties sold for in the recent past? How much did the seller originally pay for the house? Are home prices generally increasing or decreasing? Is the property in move-in condition or is it in need of substantial repairs? How long has the house been on the market? It is also critical to establish the value of the purchase to you which is generally independent of information related to the seller.

While information-gathering, you also need to explore the world of the intangible. To do that, get inside the seller's mind. What is his or her situation, needs, motivation? Is the seller under contract to purchase another property already? Is the house being sold by a relocation company that will absorb a lower price? What does the seller know about you and how will he or she use that information?

The more that you can find out about your counterparty (and the less you disclose about yourself), the better off you are. However, there is one caveat:

you should clearly understand the motivations of any party providing you with information. In a house transaction, for example, you should expect your broker to be generally honest and ethical, but less than fully transparent. Assuming your broker gets a percentage of the transaction, his or her incentive is to close as fast as possible and at as high a price as possible. You know the score going in; rely only on unbiased sources for information and heavily discount, if not completely disregard, everything else.

Determine your reservation price and know your best alternative to a negotiated agreement

To be a skillful negotiator, you must determine your reservation price before you commence formal negotiations. If you are buying, the reservation price is the maximum price that you will pay. If you are selling, the reservation price is the minimum price that you will accept. Good negotiators say to themselves: "I would like to pay around $10." Great negotiators say to themselves: "I will pay at most $10 and will walk away for even a penny more."

The reservation price is your antidote to emotional involvement in the transaction. It provides a clear signal that tells you when to disengage. You need to determine a precise reservation price *prior* to negotiating. Once you start a negotiation, you should change your reservation price only in exceptionally rare circumstances. Remember, you came into the negotiation with an information advantage drawn from unbiased sources. The negotiation process itself and your counterparty (especially in a zero sum or 'winner-take-all' transaction) are far more likely to provide you with information that is a wolf in sheep's clothing. If you hit your reservation price, then stop negotiating, period. You always have the option to cool off, gather additional information, and come back to the table with the same or a different counterparty.

The reservation price is not affected by tangible and intangible information about your counterparty. Rather, the reservation price is wholly dependent on the value of the transaction to you and on your next best alternative. The value of the transaction to you is the easy part.

The real secret sauce lies in engineering your best alternative to a negotiated agreement. In other words, put diligent effort into building your Plan B. If you want to buy a house, negotiate for two properties with different sellers instead of one. Although you will certainly improve the transaction price with every additional provider you throw into the mix, two is typically the right number to balance economic gains against time and effort. Finally, you should know when 'do nothing' is the best alternative.

Shape the game

The three strategic levers in negotiating are information, time, and power. By shaping the game, you gain control over time and power. In almost every circumstance, you can limit your sense of urgency, determine the issues on the table, and select your counterparty.

Carrying on with the home purchase example, imagine that your goal is to occupy a property by the start of the next school year, to minimize the disruption to your children. You can control the sense of urgency, by starting your information-gathering process in the winter and conducting your negotiation in the spring. Determine the issues such as price, occupancy date, financing, and so on. Finally, based on the information that you have gathered, choose which sellers to negotiate with and which ones to avoid.

Decide who will make the first offer (usually you)

If you are a moderately experienced negotiator with an information advantage in a one-off interaction, then you should make the first offer. Moreover, your offer should be as aggressive and extreme as possible, just shy of being offensive. That guidance applies to most situations that you will encounter. If you lack either the experience or the information advantage, then you can be safe allowing the other party to make the first offer, as long as you develop some defense against a powerful psychological weapon.

To understand the logic behind who should make the first offer, you need to understand the tradeoff between the psychological impact of anchoring and the information benefit of receiving the first offer.

In virtually any context, people become powerfully psychologically anchored to the first number they hear, no matter how arbitrary. If I were to ask a group of one hundred reasonably educated people in what year America gained its independence from the British, the average group response would be close to 1776, since most people know this fact. If I then asked the group when the Magna Carta was signed, the average answer for the group would be a lot closer to 1776 than the true answer even though the events have little to do with each other. (In case you forgot, the Magna Carta was originally issued in 1215 by English barons determined to protect their rights by limiting the powers of King John.) Anchoring is so powerful that even subject matter experts aware of the bias cannot, on average, protect themselves against its influence. (If you think you can, then you are guilty of overconfidence bias – but that is a horse of a different sort.)

To drive the point home, consider an experiment conducted by Michael Cotter of Grand Valley State University and James Henley of The University of Tennessee over a seven year period between 1999 and 2006. During the study, which involved 1621 total sessions, students were paired up and then asked to conduct ten separate negotiations with at least one day elapsing between each session. The researchers found that during the initial negotiation, the individual making the first offer captured on average 55% of the pie. Because most of us conduct a single negotiation with a person and then move on, it clearly pays to make the first offer.

There are, however, times when you will negotiate with a person repeatedly and the advice for that scenario is slightly different. In their experiment, Cotter and Henley found that in subsequent negotiations between the same parties, the person that waits to be the one that makes the counter offer actually does a little bit better - claiming 52% of the pie on average. What is going on? The short answer is that the counterparty in the initial negotiation has learned to defend against the anchor and actually benefits from the information contained in the first offer.

The best way to defend against an anchor is to consider disconfirming information. Such disconfirming information might be reasons why the anchor is wrong, assumptions about the other party's best alternative to a negotiated agreement, and considerations of other issues up for negotiation that are unrelated to the anchor.

Given the power of anchoring, it is easy to see why you would want to make the first offer in a negotiation in a one-off negotiation when you have an information advantage. In doing so, you will gain the benefit of anchoring the other person and prevent them from doing the same to you. Moreover, your information advantage will allow you to make an opening offer that is extreme, but just short of obscene. That way, you set yourself up to gain the largest possible value relative to your reservation price.

By making the initial proposal, you gain the anchoring advantage, but give up the information benefit of waiting for your counterparty to make the first offer. For example, you might think that $420,000 is an extreme first offer for the house you want to buy. However, there is always the chance that the seller will lead off with an even lower price.

Nevertheless, despite the information lost from not hearing your counterparty's initial offer, the anchoring effect on both you and your counterparty is so incredibly powerful that you should make the first offer in a one-off negotiation whenever you have an information advantage gleaned from other sources. The information advantage will give you confidence that your initial proposal is extreme but not crass. Hence, there will be little benefit from waiting to receive the first offer. If, however, you do not have the confidence in your information, then let the other party make the first move, do your best to ignore the anchor, and come in with an even more extreme counter-offer.

Be reticent and patient

Extremely adept negotiators are masters at using silence and patience to their advantage. Most people are uncomfortable with quiet in any social situation, including negotiations. At the very least, limiting your own chatter will prevent you from divulging information that you meant to keep to yourself. However, the most important reason to be reticent is to allow the other party to 'talk themselves' into the deal.

In my own experience, I will make a crisp and clear offer or counter-offer and then settle into a relaxed and patient silence. Nine times out of ten the person with whom I am negotiating will ultimately say "O.K., we can do that." Being patient allows you to be silent, thus downplaying any sense of urgency. In general, the person that has the most time fares best.

Read their body language, control your own

As in all forms of interaction, body language during negotiations reveals far more than words. Though not a lie detector, a non-verbal signal can be a powerful stress detector. If you spot signs of stress during a negotiation, then you have reliable evidence that your counterparty may lack full confidence in his or her last position and there is still ample room to negotiate.

To negotiate expertly, you must, at a minimum, be mindful of your own body language. Strive to control unwanted revelatory 'tells' that will benefit the other party, rather than attempting to consciously display specific physical patterns that you think may give you the upper hand.

Identify opportunities for mutual value creation

When I enrolled in a negotiation class during business school, I fancied myself a brilliant negotiator merely looking to sharpen the point on my skills. And indeed, during the first few sessions, I excelled at winner-take-all, zero-sum negotiations where the sole issue on the table was price. In the fourth class, I fell flat on my face.

In that fateful negotiation, I failed to notice that I was in a win-win scenario with multiple issues on the table that could be optimized for mutual value creation. Adept negotiators seek out issues to trade before and during the negotiation. For this to work, you need to identify factors to negotiate that have asymmetric value to you and to your counterparty. For example, a home seller might be willing to take a lower price if you commit to a faster close.

The best negotiation levers are those issues which you know are important to the other party but not important to you. Very specifically, concentrate on the factors that are important to the other party. In general, it is best to maintain the perception that factors that are essential to them are also significant to you. This allows you to make greater gains as you trade concessions. Of course, if an issue is obviously of little value to you, then full transparency is the best course of action to maintain your credibility.

Recap

Here are the concepts you can immediately apply to be a great negotiator:

- Know that everything is negotiable
- Gain an information advantage before you start negotiating
- Determine your reservation price and know your best alternative to a negotiated agreement
- Shape the game
- Decide who will make the first offer (usually you)
- Be reticent and patient
- Read the other party's body language, control your own
- Identify opportunities for mutual value creation

Chapter Seventeen:
Statistical Uncertainty

Despite having developed a strong mathematical aptitude, I entered the final year of my undergraduate education in electrical engineering with great trepidation. My nemesis was a final unmet graduation requirement to complete a course in statistics. I excelled in solving math problems that had a single, unambiguous answer. Unfortunately, I simply could not wrap my head around the idea that some problems had infinite, fuzzy solutions. In the end, I satisfied the requirement with a difficult sounding class that thankfully had very little pure statistics. That course was called "Introduction to Probability and Random Signals."

Life, luckily, was not about to let me off so easy. A few years later, I was on the verge of matriculating into business school. I am guessing that that faculty at the University of Chicago Booth School of Business knew about people like me and were not about to let us slink past with merely an introductory statistics class under our belts. Every soul that walked through their doors had to pick their poison – either "Business Statistics" or "Applied Regression Analysis". Determined to start with my head held high, I purchased an introductory statistics textbook and worked every problem from cover to cover in the summer before I started school.

A funny thing sometimes happens when you face and conquer your greatest fear. In my case, I rapidly developed a passion for statistics and went on to major in econometrics and statistics. To my great surprise, I was granted a statistics scholarship that covered a healthy chunk of my tuition. Apparently, there are not a lot of statistics geeks, even in a very quantitatively focused business school like Booth.

I offer that background merely to acknowledge my statistics bias. But, though you certainly do not need to excel in statistics to succeed in business or in life, knowing a few rudimentary concepts is extremely valuable.

Embrace Uncertainty

The greatest epiphany that I had was to embrace rather than fear variability. Uncertainty surrounds us in nature, at home, and in business. Absolute randomness is rare. Rather, seek to understand the expected outcome and the range around it (usually wider than you think)

This concept has worked its way into the professional world in the form of the very useful 80-20 rule. In 1941, management scholar Joseph Juran studied the work of Italian economist Vilfredo Pareto. Pareto had observed that 80% of the land in Italy was owned by 20% of the population. Juran honored the economist by formally coining the concept as the Pareto Principle. (Not much has changed; the top 20% of households in the United States hold 85% of the wealth. In fact, the top 1% command nearly 35% of private wealth all by themselves.)

The amazing thing about the 80-20 rule is that it allows you to stop digging when you can account for 80 percent of virtually anything. It only gets better, because you can get to that level of understanding by doing only 20 percent of the work that you would need to do to get to a total and complete answer. Unless you are a brain surgeon or a civil engineer, this rule of thumb is an risk-free and immense productivity booster. To be able to stop when you only have eighty percent of the answer requires that you embrace uncertainty; switch from thinking in terms of yes or no and instead merely accept that an outcome is likely or unlikely.

Take calculated risks

The only way to excel in business and in life is to take calculated risks. In fact, the more risks you take the better, since you will not only learn from your mistakes but will also have better odds of securing at least one big win. Nothing ventured, nothing gained.

As you venture forth, it is critical to understand that people systematically overestimate risk. Factors you should correct for that magnify perceived risk include: limited control, human made rather than natural phenomena, limited information, dreadful outcomes, lack of familiarity, and direct awareness. Moreover, we ascribe greater risk to children than to adults engaged in the exact same activity.

Indulge me in one very personal example. As a father, I am deathly concerned that one or both of my children will experience a severe spinal cord injury. This fear nearly caused me to quash my daughter's love of participating in recreational gymnastics. But, consider a few facts and figures. In the United States, there are estimated to be 40 cases of spinal cord injury per million people per year. Of these, only 16% are caused by sports and recreation accidents. Researchers in Japan provide the final piece of the puzzle. Among Japanese spinal cord injuries associated with sporting activities, 6.6% result from gymnastics. That means that the annual chance of a person experiencing a spinal cord injury in gymnastics is less than 1 in a million. To put this into perspective, the odds of dying in a motor vehicle accident in the United States are fully 340 times greater at 144 in a million. Based on the data, my fear of recreational gymnastics was completely overblown. In fact, it is really my daughter that should be worried about me.

Beware of assuming that correlation implies causality

In May 1999, a study published in the popular scientific journal *Nature* nearly put the night light industry out of business, much to the chagrin of frightened infants and toddlers everywhere. In the article, University of Pennsylvania Medical Center researchers studied the amount of ambient light that 479 subjects were exposed to during their nighttime sleep. For children from birth to two years of age, myopia – or nearsightedness – was far more prevalent in children who slept with a night light rather than in darkness. Moreover, those children whose parents left the room's light fixture on were even more likely to have eye problems later on. Parents of children with glasses must have been feeling extremely guilty for having used nightlights.

The researchers cited similar findings in studies with young chickens and outlined the likely developmental processes impacted by excessive light exposure at an early age. Though they carefully hedged their bets, the researchers teetered on the brink of implying causality when they reported: "Although it does not establish a causal link, the statistical strength of the association of night-time light exposure and childhood myopia does suggest that the absence of a daily period of darkness during early childhood is a potential precipitating factor in the development of myopia."

Fortunately, a year later, Ohio State University researchers spared millions of innocent children from the boogie man. In a larger study of 1,220 children, Karla Zadnik and her co-authors determined that ambient light during sleep does not cause nearsightedness. Instead, it turns out that nearsighted kids simply have nearsighted parents who are more likely to leave a light on than parents without vision problems, to light their own path in the middle of the night. The cause is genetic. In other words, the researchers of the initial study had found simply a correlation between ambient light and myopia, but not a causality, and thus had engendered needless guilt in many myopic parents.

Even very smart and well-meaning people fall into the trap of assuming that correlation implies causality. To contend against this, in each instance look for three other explanations. The first is an external cause. This is what was at play with the genetic cause that explained the relationship between night lights and nearsightedness. The second is known as reverse causation. For example, you might notice there are more police at larger crime scenes and incorrectly conclude that police cause crime. The third explanation is mere coincidence. Some humorous examples of this are concluding that the growth of social networking websites or hybrid automobile sales fueled the 2009 economic recession.

Recap

Here are the concepts you can immediately apply to take charge of statistical concepts :
- Embrace uncertainty
- Take calculated risks
- Beware of assuming that correlation implies causality

Chapter Eighteen: Pricing Strategy

If you have ever called a large company customer service hotline and reached a live human being, then you probably heard the representative furiously hammering away at their keyboard. In service industry parlance, they are logging a ticket that includes your contact information and your complaint into a sophisticated help desk software application. For many years, the expense of such systems meant that only the largest companies could manage customer relationships this way. However, in recent years, the Internet has served as a great equalizer allowing small and midsized business to get in on the action too. Serving them are a host of smaller help desk software vendors that provide lower cost but still reasonably powerful Internet-based solutions.

On the evening of May 18, 2010, one of these emerging players found themselves in an epic (for them) pricing pickle. The 5,000 or so loyal customers of Zendesk, whose motto really is 'Love Your Help Desk', received an email from CEO Mikkel Svane. The communication began innocently enough extolling a set of new features inspired by customer feedback. The next few paragraphs delivered the shocker. Though Zendesk's smallest customers with only one license would see no price change, everyone else would experience a minimum fifty percent and maximum two hundred percent increase! The customer uproar was, understandably, swift and scathing. Smelling blood in the water, competitors immediately went into attack mode. Not realizing the gravity of the situation, Mr. Svane commented innocently on a prominent social network that "I hope all the new sexy Zendesk features don't drown in today's noise."

In one badly calculated pricing action, Zendesk shattered the trust of their loyal early adopters. Though the company ultimately did the right thing by grandfathering pricing indefinitely to all existing customers, the damage was already done. The company survived, albeit with mud in the eye.

Pricing strategy is as much art as it is science. However, a few key guidelines will get you pointed in the right direction.

Start high

Unless you are selling a pure commodity, you should strive to launch products with high initial pricing. Many people, particularly small business owners, make the mistake of overestimating the impact that low introductory pricing will have on demand. In most circumstances, your earliest customers will be willing to pay more to get first crack at the unique benefits of your offering. Moreover, high pricing may actually stimulate demand by signaling that you are providing a premium product. If you miss the mark on the high end, then it is easy to adjust and lower prices. However, if you price too low at the beginning, then you may find yourself in the no-win situation that Zendesk faced.

Avoid radical pricing changes

It is important to get pricing as close to right as possible at initial launch. Radical changes to pricing strategies almost always end in disaster. A major change is likely to have one of three inevitable outcomes. Those clients that can pay less will take advantage of the opportunity. Those clients that must pay the same will continue on unaffected. Those clients that you expect to pay more will not. If you are lucky, those in the final bucket will simply give you a mouthful. More likely, many will vote silently with their feet and abandon you for your competition. The net result of all three behaviors is that you will lose money.

Certainly, there are exceptions to every rule. In some rare circumstances, there may be a significant untapped buying center that is unable to purchase your product without pricing strategy change. Most examples of this are of companies that offer variations of their products packaged in lower quantities or with reduced features. For instance, when Tide laundry detergent was launched in India in mid-2000, its manufacturer needed to adapt to lower household income relative to the United States. To address the opportunity, Tide was offered in a variety of sizes including single use packets targeted at rural areas. For most companies employing such a strategy, the price of the 'inferior' product should be less attractive on a relative basis as compared to the larger, full-featured offering.

Factor in costs, customers, and competition

Though you must be careful not to anchor yourself, the first thing that you should consider when setting a price point is your average total cost. Average total costs should factor in not only the variable cost of your given good or service, but also the fixed costs that you incur in the course of running your company. Average total cost establishes a minimum price point that is the dividing line between life and death for your business.

Once you establish a price floor based on costs, it is time to consider your customers. When prospects think about buying from you, the first thing they consider is the potential value they can realize. However, customers typically will not pay the full value they expect to gain from your offering. They require compensation for the risk they take in buying from you.

To make this more concrete, consider a purchase decision that companies face every day. Most businesses, whether selling to consumers or to other businesses, spend considerable dollars to buy lists of prospects that are fed into direct marketing campaigns. Though figures vary widely, a typical response rate to an unqualified prospect campaign is about one percent. However, just getting a response is only a small part of the battle. Of prospects that respond to a phone, post mail, or email offer, perhaps five percent of them will actually make a purchase. If the product sells for $2,000, then the value of the contact information for a single unqualified prospect is $2,000 times one percent times five percent. That works out to a value to the customer of just one crisp dollar.

Since the list buyer made a number of assumptions based on typical industry standards, their willingness to pay would be a decent amount lower to account for the very likely possibility that response rates and conversion rates will turn out lower than expected. Recalling the work of Kahneman and Tversky from the chapter on change management, most people require a factor of two times return on investment. Hence, in this example, the list buyer's willingness to pay for an incremental unqualified set of contact information is likely a mere fifty cents.

Now that you have considered your costs and your customers' willingness to pay, there is one more thing to factor in to your pricing decision - the dreaded competition. Though companies hate to admit it, there are generally a few competitors lurking in their waters that offer a more or less fungible solution. This is true for both goods and services. To keep yourself in business, you should carefully monitor your competitor's list prices as well as their realized effective prices.

When most people perform competitive analysis in the context of pricing strategy, they stop at examining external competition. However, to avoid devastating errors, you should also look at the impact that a new product or pricing action will have on other offerings in your portfolio. Take care to set a price that will not cannibalize your existing business.

Recap

Here are the concepts you can immediately apply to become a skilled pricing strategist:

- Start high
- Avoid radical pricing changes
- Factor in costs, customers, and competition

Chapter Nineteen: Mergers and Acquisitions

In the nine year period spanning June 2001 to June 2010, International Business Machines Corporation (IBM) acquired 92 companies for in excess of $25 billion dollars. If you are lucky enough to work for a juggernaut that averages ten acquisitions per year, then you can probably skip this chapter. However, the rest of us are unlikely to have a finely tuned merger machine humming away at corporate headquarters. Instead, acquisition due diligence and post-merger integration will likely be tackled by a cross-functional team of smart, well intentioned people who at least want to look like they know what they are doing.

The statistics on merger success rates are sobering. This has been true for decades, as evidenced by everything from Harvard professor Michael Porter's 1987 assertion that fifty to sixty percent of acquisitions result in failure to McKinsey & Company's 2004 calculation that only twenty-three percent of acquisitions have a positive return on investment. If you define success by a lower standard, that acquired companies continue to operate within the acquired company or as a divestiture, then the prognosis does improve a little. Unfortunately, that yardstick measures mere Pyrrhic victories.

If you are thrown into the M&A battlefield, there are a few vital recommendations that will improve your odds of survival and give you a fighting chance at success.

Choose acquisition targets that extend your core value proposition

Integration challenges grow exponentially with deal size and business focus relative to your existing organization. Consequently, you are likely to realize the best results by acquiring smaller firms that reinforce or extend your existing strategy. This means that you must identify the concrete, incremental value proposition the target company brings.

Logically, the most fruitful acquisitions involve purchases that increase production or sales capacity. A close second are deals to acquire a new product that you can sell to your existing customers. Be very honest with yourself about the capacity of your existing sales force to absorb the new offering.

Things get significantly harder when the value proposition involves buying into a new channel to sell your product. After all, if those prospective customers had found your product valuable, you probably would have built a way to access them a long time ago. Finally, you should avoid pure diversification plays, unless you work for a holding company with financial engineering expertise and low-cost access to capital. Offering a new product to a new set of customers amounts to nothing more than gambling with your investors' money.

The concrete value proposition for the acquisition should be translated into rigorously quantified drivers of value creation. These drivers will typically include a schedule for cost reduction, financial engineering including tax benefits, and revenue projections.

Anticipate and manage acquisition risks

All acquisitions carry risk. However, risk alone should not be a deterrent. Rather, you have an opportunity and an obligation to identify key risk factors and develop plans to mitigate them. During the acquisition process, most people take a functional approach, an excellent start. Specifically, you may create teams to explore issues around merging information technology, production, sales, human resources, legal requirements, and so on. Unfortunately, too many buyers ignore the softer risk factors that fall between functional gaps. Crucially, really get to know the cultures of both companies and what is likely to happen when they intermix. This will enable you to proactively address issues that arise. For example, your company might be dominated by a fact-based decision making culture. If you acquire a people-focused culture, then do not expect your new colleagues to be swayed by purely rational arguments. They will need time to build trust and are likely to drag their feet in sharing developing problems; so, motivate, inspire, and prove yourself trustworthy.

In addition to the softer side of internal issues, you should similarly plan for external reactions to the acquisition. How will your customers react? How will their customers react? What is your brand strategy?

Engineer your post-merger integration strategy

If there is one recurring theme in engineering successful acquisitions, it is planning, planning, planning. As articulated earlier, proper planning includes integration milestones and goals that span functional and 'softer' cultural and customer issues. Since you cannot anticipate every eventuality, establish a clear escalation process for unforeseen problems. For that to be effective, you will need to reserve financial and intellectual capacity for frequent problem solving and future investments.

During acquisitions, it is vital to provide clear and unambiguous leadership by selecting the new management team early on. The team should include a passionate, execution driven integration leader with past merger experience, strong incentives, and comprehensive decision making authority. Even if you do not have a leader with past merger experience, all hope is not lost. In that instance, you should pony up the extra money to bring in outside consultants to help engineer the details.

In all service-based businesses, and even most manufacturing businesses, the key asset that you are purchasing is people and their associated intellectual capital. Since acquisitions are a time of turmoil for the acquirer and the target, one of your most important early responsibilities is to give everyone affected clarity on their new roles, responsibilities, and reporting structure. You want people to spend as little time as possible worrying about their job security and their sense of purpose in the combined enterprise. Though the leadership team may feel it has a respectable idea of what is going on, everyone else has the impression, rightly or wrongly, that they do not have enough information. Hence, plan to repeatedly communicate the post merger strategic vision to employees.

Though words are by far the most important, money also matters. Remember to provide incentives to retain key employees across all important functions in the target. A useful best practice is to define a three tier structure. The first tier includes the ten to fifteen percent of star talent who should have the strongest courtship and retention incentives. Bear in mind that not all management is star talent. Moreover, many major contributors work in individual contributor roles. The second tier includes the dedicated bunch who are collectively, but not individually, key to the ultimate success of the merger. Finally, the third tier includes people that you expect to part ways within a well specified amount of time in order to realize cost savings.

This degree of over-communication should extend beyond employees to your customers. Customers on both sides of the aisle will grapple with uncertainty. Competitors will take advantage of this ambiguity and your higher than normal level of distraction by intensifying their marketing activities. Anticipating this, develop a clear strategy to retain existing customers. Also, be realistic that customer attrition rates – especially at the target company – are likely to degrade.

During the due diligence phase, you established a measurable set of value drivers. Those defined what great looks like for the purchase. As the integration proceeds, institute formal tracking of the acquisition's performance against those goals. In most instances, a monthly review with the company operating committee and quarterly review with the board of directors is sufficient. Beyond keeping everyone honest, these reviews keep people focused on what needs to be accomplished.

Recap

Here are the concepts you can immediately apply to become great at acquisition due diligence and post-merger integration:

- Choose acquisition targets that extend your core value proposition
- Anticipate and manage acquisition risks
- Engineer your post-merger integration strategy

Chapter Twenty: Corporate Strategy

Corporate strategy boils down to the broadly coordinated and highly focused initiatives that will have substantial impact on revenue growth or cost containment. Your mission is to determine the essential actions to take in an atmosphere of limited labor and capital resources.

As you plan to embark on a new strategic direction, spend adequate time thinking how the chess board is going to evolve at least a few moves forward. Ask yourself how your employees, your customers, and your competitors will react. In some instances, you may need to add anticipated supplier and government reactions to your analysis. As a good steward of your company and the planet, comprehend the environmental and social impact of your actions.

Many successful strategic directions that you can take, any of your competitors could replicate. If it makes sense after careful consideration to travel that path, then by all means do so, picking the low hanging fruit first. Ultimately, however, the greatest strategies take your company in a direction that reinforces your strengths in such a way that competitors cannot follow.

Identify the major levers that drive your business

The best way to identify to the strategic objectives that matter, is to determine the major levers that drive your business. Some levers, like the cost of commodity inputs including labor, are mostly out of your control. Other levers can be tuned through concerted action. In most organizations, the primary drivers are incremental investment in initiatives that drive growth, in contrast to those that affect operational effectiveness or cost.

Regardless of your organization size, you have a responsibility to continually evaluate where your business is performing well and where it is not. Larger enterprises can do this using business intelligence dashboards that sit on top of data warehouses. Smaller companies have enough information to do this as well. You should explore how your business is doing in various major customer firmographic or demographic segments. You should know which of your products are growing, which are declining, and how much of the total available market you have captured.

If you sit through a business school course on corporate strategy, you would likely learn about four major ways to grow. These include investing large sums of money in vertical integration, diversification, product innovation, or geographic expansion. Rather than retread this well traveled landscape, I encourage you to think about major drivers that rely more on effective coordination than they do on expenditure. There are at least three places to find initiatives with that kind of profile.

The first is how you bring your products to market. Major levers there are actions that you can take to either retain or to upgrade existing clients. By way of example, if you crunch client retention statistics in the information services business, you find a pretty obvious result. Engagement drives retention. If a client spends time reading a document, then he or she renews at a higher rate. If he or she takes the time to meet with you face to face, the rate grows higher. Booking a hotel room and getting on an airplane to attend your conference, boosts retention even higher. On top of total engagement, there is a strong recency bias at play. You can find a window of time toward the end of a contract period that has the greatest impact on renewal. In your business, collect a lot of data and hire a statistician to tell you what matters to your clients.

In addition to optimizing retention and upgrades, another product direction you can take is selling existing products to new buyers and new products to existing buyers. Though geographic expansion is one example of the former, there are many other avenues such as expanding in a focused way into new vertical markets. The worst thing you can do is sell a new product to a new buyer. Avoid that strategy at all costs.

The second place to find low-cost, high-reward strategic initiatives is in sales effectiveness. This topic is covered in depth in another chapter in this book.

Among the various knobs to turn, hiring and compensation will have the greatest effect.

The third place to explore is your marketing activities. Finding new ways to generate and pre-qualify leads can have an amazing influence on your revenue growth. Most sales professionals abhor cold calling, so apply an automation process such as Webinars that filters the leads. In addition, systematically measure customer loyalty so that you can maximize promoters and minimize detractors. Remember, if you ask customers for feedback, then you must ensure that you have allocated the time and money to fully address or at least empathetically respond to their concerns.

Launch strategic initiatives in a coordinated fashion

After you have identified a reasonably comprehensive set of growth levers for your business, it is time to get down to brass tacks. Since new strategic initiatives involve human beings that have constrained capacity for change, the number one thing is to focus. To keep yourself honest in the selection process and in measuring outcomes, rank order projects by forecasted return on investment multiplied by expected probability of success. In the end, you should land preferably one but as many as three critical initiatives.

The most important decision that you will make is assigning a single, fully focused, and fully accountable project leader. Broad executive support all the way up to the CEO is critical to success. However, "C"-level executives should not be project leaders unless the project is their sole focus. Working in concert with the larger team, the project leader should have full decision making authority over the required training, tools, and management systems that need to be created to inspect and correct as the program marches forward.

Successful kick-off meetings are crucial to coordinating large projects. A strong statement of the problem that motivates the emotional and the rational brain will help promote commitment. Additionally, participants will want to know the concrete business objective so that they know what they are fighting for and when they are done. When the meeting is over, important stakeholders should have a clear understanding of the scope of the project, the work-streams they own, and the expected timeline for progress.

With a major project, define a series of project phases. In many instances, you can implement changes as each phase is completed. This is a variation on the valuable 'execute and iterate' theme. In other cases, you have the option to develop in phases and then release all at once.

Right size your budget to succeed

To succeed, major strategic initiatives need adequate capital and labor resources that have to come from somewhere. To make room, you have three options.

The first is to ask yourself if there is anything on the plate that you can do differently and more efficiently. Since you are likely to be busy and too close to your own processes, this is at least one area where outside consultants can add value.

The second is to ask if new initiatives have to be so big. In many circumstances, you can find ways to reduce scope that have minimal impact on the ultimate return on investment. Reducing scope has the added benefit of increasing the probability of success.

The final task is exploring if you can make the plate bigger. For most companies, this is the last avenue pursued since it requires raising capital.

Recap

Here are the concepts you can immediately apply to become a talented business strategist:
- Identify the major levers that drive your business
- Launch strategic initiatives in a coordinated fashion
- Right size your budget to succeed

PART FOUR:

INNOVATION

Chapter Twenty One:
Client Interviewing

Whether you are developing a new product or managing an existing one, your ability to learn from your clients and prospects will be the deciding factor in your success. The techniques in this chapter will help you extract the maximum amount of information in the minimum amount of time.

Develop and refine the interview guide

As with pretty much everything else, the single characteristic that most sharply delineates exceptional interviewers from average ones is the amount of time spent planning. To plan effectively, start with the goal and work backward. Identify the fundamental decisions, often framed as tradeoffs, your team will need to make. Only then can you form questions that provide unambiguous answers to the most pressing issues.

I once worked on a product development project where the goal was to drive revenue growth for a quantitative information product. This product was a database of market forecast information that clients could use to make fact-based decisions on which new markets to target. My team expected revenue growth from three sources:winning new clients, increasing purchases by existing clients, and improving retention among existing clients. With a development budget in hand, we set out to determine which new features and enhancements would have the biggest revenue impact as we migrated the product from an offline database to a rich online experience.

Consider just one feature – online data visualization. At the outset of the project, there was raging internal debate about the importance of providing clients the ability to generate rich graphics through our web experience. Of course, as a complex feature, this would consume considerable time and money, forcing us to drop other product attributes from scope. Moreover, this was an emotionally charged (and entirely opinion based) issue. In short, it was perfect fodder for inclusion in a client interview.

When we asked clients to rate this feature and several others, we learned that users on the whole just wanted pure data and lots of it. These largely technical clients preferred to analyze the data using their own charting software. With this information in hand, we were able to significantly lower the project risk and focus on features that would delight our customers.

Time is precious during an interview so you need to make every question count. I have seen many interview guides that ask for information that could be obtained in advance through other means. Some examples include probing for biographical information ('What is your job title?') or for usage information ('When did you last log in to our system?'). If your systems do not provide this information, then seek only the minimum necessary and move as fast as possible to the heart of the interview.

People new to interviewing tend to draft overly quantitative and overly long question guides. If you must, you can ask at most five 'rate on a scale of 1 to 10' style questions in a thirty minute interview. Such questions sometimes irritate the person you are interviewing since it makes the discussion feel more like a survey rather than a conversation. In fact, many people, especially senior executives, will refuse to provide a quantitative response . In their wisdom, they are trying to protect you from yourself; they know the color commentary matters far more than the rating. In those circumstances, it is perfectly acceptable and expected that you form an estimate and not probe for a number. For those people that do give you a number, always follow their response by asking two more questions. The first is why they assigned that rating. The second, a crucial best practice, is to ask what would be a ten.

To expand a bit more on controlling interview length, you can develop extremely effective interview guides that have as few as three or four questions. If you are trying to develop a new product, you can ask three simple questions. First, what do you value? Second, if we deliver the specific feature you value, how will that drive success in your job? Third, if we deliver the specific feature you value, will it make you more likely to buy?

The "what do you value question" has its proponents and its detractors. Occasionally, you will be in unchartered territory with a product or service that is both new and experiential. Henry Ford faced this in the early days of the automobile and advised "If I'd asked my customers what they wanted, they'd have said a faster horse." You have two options in this circumstance. First, if your concept is far enough along, then you can assess the value of specific product attributes. Second, you can explore a variation on the 'what keeps you up at night?' theme. To prevent eye-rolling, rephrase the question into something not quite so cliché. One possible approach is to ask: 'What are the critical issues that you are currently facing?' Then, you should probe for what they do today as a work-around and what they would prefer as a long term solution. Another approach is to ask a person what defines success in their current role. This most certainly fuels insomnia. Yet another variation is to have people identify the most valuable activities they currently do and to follow up by asking which of those they would be willing to offload or outsource.

There is a parallel set of streamlined interview questions for an existing product. One, what were your expectations when you first purchased our product? Two, which of your expectations were and were not met? Three, will you renew and why? Four, what would you change? The final question can be further refined by probing clients to describe their ideal.

Once you complete a draft of the interview guide, you should expect to spend several painstaking iterations refining the questions. Mercilessly remove any questions that do not provide guidance on key decisions that further your overall objective. Shorter is always better. Also, regardless of whether the survey is qualitative or quantitative, pilot the survey qualitatively with a few individuals before you launch to work out any final kinks.

Source interview candidates

In one-on-one qualitative interviewing, simply finding good candidates is the longest lead time component of the process. Hence, to ensure your success, start recruiting and scheduling early. In fact, an efficient best practice is to source interviewees at the same time you start developing the interview guide.

The answers that you get in your study undoubtedly will depend on the people to whom you talk; so, segment them. For example, say you are conducting a study to determine the best practices of effective sales managers. Rather than asking the manager's managers to rate performance based on opinion, you should actually determine which sales managers are most effective based on objective, unbiased data. A best practice from an underperforming individual may not be what it seems.

Candidate selection is especially important when talking to customers and prospects. Generally, the lowest hanging fruit are existing customers, as they are more likely to take your call and you have their contact information at hand. If you pick only there, then at least make sure to separate your profitable customers from those you would like to fire (the last thing you want to do is to develop enhancements that will drive away loyal customers and lock in unprofitable ones.) However, you can and should go a step further. Make the effort to interview prospects as well as lost customers.

Additional considerations often arise during client interview selection. Specifically, be careful to not disrupt an active sales cycle. Before you solicit a client in this circumstance, reach out to the assigned sales executive to make sure that your discussion will not slow down a win-back or renewal opportunity. In my experience, sales people appreciate the courtesy and are all too happy to have another person engage their client.

Elicit attitudes and ideas

Though this chapter is titled "Client Interviewing", remarkable interviewers are more precisely focused on eliciting. The main difference is that interviewing ends with merely understanding the answers to the scripted questions that you have posed. In contrast, eliciting draws forth attitudes and ideas When you elicit, the person to whom you are talking should be doing eighty to ninety percent of the talking.

To maximize the value of the live interview time, you should make it a practice to send the interview guide or any supporting material to the interviewee in advance of your session. This will save much wasted time explaining background information and allow the individual to think through his or her answers before speaking. If you are paranoid about competitors getting hold of your interview guide, then you are worried about the wrong thing. First of all, if your competition has strong relationships with your clients, then they are going to find out what you are planning by word of mouth. Second, if leaking your interview guide to competitors dulls your competitive edge, then you should think about working on projects that enhance your unique differentiation and are strategically hard for your competitor to replicate.

Interviewees will provide more insightful feedback if you explain your goals upfront. In addition, they will benefit from knowing what they stand to gain. For example, if you are evaluating a set of enhancements to an existing product without a price change, then let the individual know. For many folks, being able to provide creative input, and then seeing those ideas come to life, is reward enough.

With time pressure and a need to have the interviewee dominate the conversation, you should seek to glean answers in as few questions as possible. Unsurprisingly, word choice determines efficacy. . The least efficient questions begin with "how" or "what". Questions commencing with "why" are much more revealing. Asking a succession of deeper and deeper 'why's' can be very illuminating. The ultimate question starter is "what if". A query formed this way allows the interviewee to imagine themselves in a future where the topic of discussion is a reality.

Where possible, you should guide the person with whom you are speaking to provide actual anecdotal answers rather than pure aspirations. I can vividly recall interviewing an information technology professional about features associated with a new product. While she provided feedback enthusiastically, I could sense that her language was somehow too conceptual. When prompted to describe how she would use the product in her own organization, she quickly replied 'Oh, this offering is not right for my team.' She viewed herself as a valuable adjunct (and eager to please) member of the development team when what we really needed was her candid reaction as a potential user.

As you interview, you should be as unbiased as possible. You must disconnect yourself emotionally from your company and think of yourself as an objective third party consultant. To that end, resist the temptation to defend yourself, sell, educate, or problem solve. I once conducted an interview where the other party articulated the value proposition of our business as influence peddling. This touched a nerve at the core of my personal values and our corporate identity. However, that was the person's candid opinion and this was not the forum to challenge them. If you uncover a similar issue, or a more innocuous, though still important, service problem, it can always be addressed responsibly after the interview.

As a matter of respect, manage the discussion so that you end on time. An amazingly effective best practice is asking the following question about five or more minutes before the end of the interview: "Is there anything that I forgot to ask?" This query usually opens the floodgates of creativity. When you ask this question to the right person at the right time, you will get out-of-the-box ideas that can transform your business.

Pan where the gold is

I have had the good fortune to coach people to become skillful interviewers. Almost without fail, when these individuals begin the process, they start with a perceived need to get through every question on an interview guide. Unfortunately, this means giving short shrift to any individual topic of discussion.

A better approach is to view interviewing like panning for gold. If you are working a riverbed and hit the mother lode, then you keep panning in that spot all day and all night. In the world of interviewing, that means that you should only shift gears if the person is way off topic. It is always better to go extremely deep in an area for which an interviewee shows insight and passion, even if it means not getting to some of the other prepared questions. You can always cover other portions of the interview guide with other people if there are questions left unanswered.

Send thank you notes or gifts

Interviewing people provides an opportunity for you to demonstrate grace and charm and even to build new relationships. To that end, you should make it a practice to send thank you notes or gifts in a timely fashion. Merely thanking someone for their time is better than not thanking them at all. An off the charts show of gratitude should capture specifics of the creative ideas the individual provided and should articulate the value those ideas have to you and to your business.

Recap

Here are the concepts you can immediately apply to become a great interviewer:

- Develop and refine the interview guide
- Source interview candidates
- Elicit attitudes and ideas
- Pan where the gold is
- Send thank you notes or gifts

Chapter Twenty Two: Brainstorming

The mere mention of the Great Depression conjures thoughts of universal economic collapse exemplified by breadlines and soup kitchens. However, a handful of companies including Procter and Gamble and Chevrolet managed to survive, and even thrive, during the 1929 to 1939 economic meltdown. Though the successful companies come from a variety of industries, they share one very important characteristic; they ramped up advertising expenditures while their peers tightened their belt buckles and fell into a slow death spiral Enough Procter and Gambles and Chevrolets existed to enable the print and radio advertising industry to expand by leaps and bounds.

The burgeoning advertising industry led to modern brainstorming as we know it. To meet the increasing demand for ever more differentiated and innovative concepts, the industry needed to find a way to dramatically increase productivity. A man named Alex Faickney Osborn had the answer. Born in May 1888, Osborn founded the BBDO agency (he's the "O") that is now a jewel in the crown of media behemoth Omnicom. More importantly, A.F. Osborn is regarded as having singularly invented the concept of brainstorming to maximize the generation of advertising ideas. Having introduced the technique for internally at BBDO earlier in his career, Osborn originally shared his gift with the world in the 1948 book "Your Creative Power" and expanded on the concept in the 1957 book "Applied Imagination." Among other things, his work established four prescriptive rules for successful brainstorming that remain in widespread use today. The rules are:
1. Aim to generate the maximum quantity of ideas
2. Avoid criticizing any ideas
3. Attempt to improve upon previously generated ideas
4. Encourage the generation of radical ideas

Over the years, social scientists have had ample opportunity to explore the nooks and crannies of Osborn's theories. Though a few intrepid explorers have attempted to study idea quality, it is practically impossible to measure with certainty. Consequently, most researchers measure the effectiveness of brainstorming based on Mr. Osborn's first rule - generating the maximum quantity of ideas.

First thing's first. The dirty little secret about group brainstorming is that it does not work – at least when the yardstick for success measures the sheer volume of distinct ideas generated. A great many researchers have found that productivity drops as group size increases. Hence, it is far better to have five people brainstorm individually and then merge their findings than to stick all of them in a room together. This is due to a combination of people wasting valuable time interrupting each other and people holding back ideas for various social and psychological reasons.

Despite evidence of foolhardiness, group brainstorming is pervasive and highly valued. But, why? I believe there are two very good reasons. The first is that idea quantity is not the only thing that matters. Idea quality is important too. It is hard to compare the effectiveness of individual versus group brainstorming on idea quality. Remember Osborn's third rule, which is to improve upon previously generated ideas during a brainstorming session. If you have ever bounced your ideas off someone else, then you know the power of having more than one set of eyeballs on a problem.

The second reason that group brainstorming remains pervasive is perhaps even more important. It has nothing to do with quality or quantity. For an idea to truly be judged as great, it needs to make the journey from brain to successful implementation. By synthesizing ideas in a group setting, great managers instill shared ownership and commitment. This buy-in is well worth the price of a few less ideas.

If you are going to run a group brainstorming process, here are some essential tips for success.

Set the environment so that people clear their minds

When people walk into my office, the first thing they notice is its operating room sterility. My gleaming desk, free of photos and paper, is surrounded on all sides by equally gleaming whiteboard walls. Creative types would tell me I have it all wrong. I have to admit, they are probably correct;in fact, one of the most creative people I know has crafted an environment that is diametrically opposite. For better or worse, his office is so different from everyone else's that it is a frequent topic of office gossip. He has turned off the stack overhead florescent light and basks instead in the glow of warm desktop lamps. Music plays softly in the background. His walls are adorned with serene landscape photography. All of this pays off for him since he is the one that frequently comes up with the 'damn, why didn't I think of that' idea.

Just as it is for my creative colleague, a warm and slightly different setting is highly conducive to productive brainstorming. If you can afford the time and expense, then it is a good idea to run brainstorming sessions at offsite locations. This takes away the emotional intensity of corporate conference rooms. More importantly, it puts people in the right mindset by removing the distracting possibility of leaving for a few minutes to take an important call.

If you cannot leave the confines of your office building, then you still have many options to alter the setting. Start by rearranging tables and chairs. Though some social scientist has no doubt studied optimal configurations, it is most likely the case that the important thing is just that the arrangement is different. You can further alter the setting by dimming the lighting even if subtly, or like my colleague, playing music.

One of the more interesting though intuitive findings of brainstorming research is that the presence of an authority figure in the room has a strong negative impact on idea generation. When the boss is around, employees take less risk and are therefore generally reluctant to offer radical ideas. Hence, if you are the boss, get out of the room. Have a third party facilitator or qualified member of your staff run the show.

Share Osborn's Rules and an aggressive quantity goal

In 2008, Washington & Jefferson College researcher Robert C. Litchfield set out to determine whether or not Osborn's rules actually matter. He was wise to do so since there is a great deal of entrenched conventional wisdom that is either a waste of time or outright destructive. To answer the question, Litchfield gave 264 undergraduate students a version of what is known as the "thumbs problem." Specifically, all participants were given ten minutes to "generate ideas about the benefits and difficulties that would arise if everyone born after 2006 had an extra thumb on each hand."

Good thing for us and for him, the professor was actually interested in two things. The first was the impact of Osborn's rules and the second was the importance of providing a specific but difficult idea quantity goal. To study these two effects individually and in combination, Litchfield divided the participants into for four categories. Though each individual brainstormed in isolation, he or she was given one of four sets of additional instructions.

The first two clusters were given either Osborn's rules or a vague quantity goal. Those with the vague quantity objective were told: "Your goal will be to do your best to generate as many ideas about the "thumbs problem' as you can within ten minutes." The vague quantity goal folks did the worst in the entire study, generating only 7.3 ideas on average in the ten minutes allotted. Not far ahead, the Osborn's rules only crew came up with 7.9 on average. These results are statistically equivalent given their means, sample sizes, and standard deviations. In other words, you are going to get the same rather poor result if you provide your brainstorming team with either a vague quantity goal or Osborn's rules. Good thing, then, that Professor Litchfield had two more tests up his sleeve.

For his third test, Litchfield tried something different. He gave sixty seven individuals a specific and difficult quantity goal, but did not include Osborn's rules. Fifteen years previously, two other researchers had determined that sixty-five ideas represented an aggressive but attainable goal for a twenty-five minute version of the "thumbs problem." Pro-rating this for a ten minute task works out to twenty-six ideas. Litchfield gave his subjects an even more aggressive objective of thirty ideas. In his words, "I rounded up on the side of difficulty." This group outperformed the other two thinking up 8.7 ideas on average.

Professor Litchfield's last and final test is where things get exciting. The last group was given both Osborn's brainstorming rules and the 30-idea aggressive quantity goal. Their explicit instructions were "Previous research indicates that it is possible to generate 30 ideas in 10 min. Please try to generate 30 ideas in this session." This cohort trounced the other three, delivering 10.3 ideas on average in ten minutes. (Incidentally, the best any of the 264 students did was 25 ideas, just shy of the aggressive expectation).

What was the Litchfield study's crucial takeaway? To get the most out of your brainstorming session, share both Osborn's rules and a specific yet difficult quantity goal. Since every situation is different and you are not going to have the luxury of having someone else figure out what difficult looks like, you can assume that 25 ideas, give or take, for every ten minutes is sufficiently aggressive.

Minimize group size

As highlighted earlier, larger brainstorming groups are less productive than smaller ones due to a variety of social and psychological impediments. Consequently, you have a few options to catalyze idea generation. The first option is to ask individuals to 'pre-brainstorm' so that they can hand in a written copy of their ideas at the start of the session. Providing anonymity is useful as that encourages more radical ideas, albeit at the expense of individual recognition.

Since people are busy, 'pre-brainstorming' may be a lot to ask. Fortunately, you have at least one more good option. Rather than brainstorm in a large group, you can ask people to brainstorm in smaller groups of between two and four individuals and then reconvene to aggregate ideas.

In the extreme, you can have an initial period of silence in the room where people jot their ideas down on paper. As awkward as a partially silent meeting seems, research has proven that people generate a greater volume of ideas when they write them down rather than vocalize them.

Provide visual idea capture

I can vividly remember the most frustrating brainstorming meeting that I ever sat in. This meeting had about thirty people sitting in a large, high-tech conference room with another ten participants on a phone conference line. Compounding the exasperation for everyone involved, the facilitator was one of the individuals on the phone. However, far and away the most disappointing aspect of this experience was that there was no one visually capturing ideas as they were generated. That our ideas were falling on deaf ears was confirmed by the fact that a follow up summary of ideas created in the session was never shared.

When you run a brainstorming meeting, make sure that you do three things. First, appoint a person to act as a scribe for ideas, letting everyone know who this person is. Second, have the scribe capture ideas in a way that is visible to the entire team. Options include using whiteboard or projecting on a screen. Third, send a summary of the ideas generated to the entire team soon after the brainstorming session.

Recap

Here are the concepts you can immediately apply to become great at running brainstorming meetings:

- Set the environment so that people clear their minds
- Share and follow Osborn's Rules and an aggressive quantity goal
- Minimize group size
- Provide visual idea capture

Chapter Twenty Three:
Entrepreneurship

In late 1999, times were good for twenty four year-old John Friess. He was living in Los Angeles and pulling down a decent wage in a product marketing role. His employer, a contractor to Kozmo.com, was helping to revolutionize the retail experience by providing Internet consumers with instant gratification. Kozmo.com offered one-hour point–to-point delivery of small ticket items like movies and groceries in eleven major cities in the United States. With Kozmo. com headed toward what seemed like a near certain and red-hot initial public offering, John looked forward to celebrating the holidays with his new fiancée. Then, John got a call from his older brother that changed the course of his professional life.

John's brother Mark, a second year medical student, was watching the dot-com bubble build and wanted in on the action. Though they did not have a concrete business idea, the brothers spent the next couple of months brainstorming ideas for a startup in healthcare technology that could make a difference in people's lives. Ultimately an idea struck them.

When he went on hospital rounds, Mark noticed that physicians spent precious little time with patients – on average only about seven minutes. Patients needed a lot more information to give them comfort and reassurance. Compounding the problem, many doctors could not communicate directly with non-English speaking patients. Seeing an unmet need, Mark and John decided their business would provide multilingual healthcare videos streamed over the Internet into hospitals and doctors' offices. The clips would provide patients with valuable information on the diseases they were diagnosed with, treatment options, and what to expect during and after medical procedures.

A great idea is only the smallest part of the battle. If John and Mark were going to make their concept fly, they would need to give up their day jobs. Mark went to the dean of his medical school at Oregon Health & Sciences University and asked for a two-year sabbatical figuring that they could build and sell the business in a flash. John took a comparable risk, quitting his job and moving back in with his parents in Oregon. Fortunately, his fiancée stuck with him. They started out with little money in the bank and a mere ten-thousand dollars in seed capital from Mark's trusting father-in-law. In March 2000, wired.MD was incorporated by its first two unpaid employees.

The Friess brother's dream of a quick and lucrative exit did not last long. In the six day period from March 10 to March 15, 2000, the dot-com era came to an abrupt end as the NASDAQ lost nearly nine percent. Venture capitalists scoffed at the idea of streaming Internet video, telling the boys they should stick to physical media like DVDs and video cassettes.

Despite the darkening clouds overhead, they went on to raise another $100,000 in September 2000. Even in a bust, companies with real products that have tangible benefits can thrive. All told, they raised a total of $2.9 million. After nearly eight years with each of the founders logging 3000 hours annually, wired. MD produced 410 patient education videos in eight languages sold in 48 states. On January 15, 2008, the company with its thirteen employees was sold for $7.4 million to MediMedia USA. Kozmo.com, which by comparison had raised $250 million only to fail spectacularly in April 2001, was but a distant memory.

I asked John what advice he would give himself if he could send a letter back in time to his 24-year-old self. His lesson number one: entrepreneurs need to participate in a peer mentoring support group where they can share advice, resources, and human networks. He added with a mix of humor and earnestness, "Sometimes you just want to know that there is someone out there that is worse off than you." To give other entrepreneurs what he lacked starting out, John co-created Starve Ups, a not-for-profit organization that facilitates peer networking in a confidential, founders-only environment.

John's second lesson is that you need to have the appropriate level of financial resources. The problem of too little capital is obvious. However, John rails against over-capitalization as an even greater evil. He may just be onto something. Cambridge Associates, an investment research house, reported that ten-year annualized United States venture capital returns for the period ending June 30, 2010 were a depressing negative 4.2%.

His third and final lesson is that everyone in the company, not just the founders, needs to be "selling, selling, selling" every day. He added, "In the end, if you are selling well, you will find a way to get past your problems."

Every entrepreneur would likely give their younger incarnation slightly different advice. Below, I have captured a set of principles that would make a compelling addition to any time capsule.

Find an idea that inspires you, your team, and your customers

In at least one respect, the Friess brothers did something that would make most entrepreneurs cringe. Rather than starting out with a concrete idea, John and Mark seemed to be as motivated by the opportunity to ride the early Internet wave as they were by developing innovative healthcare technology. The more common recipe for success is having a BIG idea that you are passionate about. However, they ultimately got their bearings just before they pulled the trigger on wired. MD with a concept that inspired them and would change people's lives for the better.

Though focus is critical, successful entrepreneurs also share the wisdom that you should expand your mind as you mull over your overall idea. Think of your initial solution as the first stage in a larger journey. Instead of defining your business by what it is today, define it in terms of where it is going.

For instance, wired.MD's initial product was appropriately laser focused on delivering healthcare video content purchased by doctors for patients in a clinical environment. They could have broadened their ultimate scope in several ways. One would have been to serve the greater needs of physicians seeking healthcare information within their specialty. This might include access to journal articles, reviews of emerging drugs and medical devices, and peer forums.

Another direction would have been to expand direct patient access to healthcare information beyond the doctor's office or hospital room. This could be composed of services like doctor moderated communities, peer forums, physician referrals, and comprehensive guides to symptoms and treatments. They could have taken things one step further by providing 24-hour access to online medical professionals to answer nagging medical questions when one's own doctor is unavailable. (This was the path taken by JustAnswer Corporation.)

In the long term, it is best to position yourself as addressing a societal need that can improve the lives of people or the planet. However, starting out, many entrepreneurs recommend that you position against an industry leader. In the case of wired.MD back in 2000, that would have meant finding niches that Healtheon/WebMD had not yet conquered. Positioning against a leader allows the larger entity's brand equity to wear off on you and helps customers grasp what you are doing.

Balance the what, the how, and the why

The overwhelming majority of entrepreneurs possess deep technical expertise whether it is baking cupcakes or writing software code. They thrive on the adrenaline rush of their craft. Unfortunately, failing to transcend the "what" is a death trap for any business, especially a fledgling one. Great entrepreneurs build a team of A-player technicians to convert their dreams into reality. Hire great people that can execute on everything that matters strategically and then outsource everything else.

The biggest first step for most entrepreneurs is making the leap from chief cupcake maker to manager of the bakers. This is the step that elevates individuals from the "what" to the "how." As a manager, your job is to set and control scope. Any reasonable scope should include a set of key milestones and at least some detail of the tasks needed to get there. The result is that great entrepreneurs deliver the "how" by architecting business processes and systems that allow ordinary people to deliver extraordinary value to customers.

If technicians possess the "what" skill and managers possess the "how" skill, then leaders possess the "why" skill. Fortunately, this is a step that most people find easier to take. Though leadership is many things, a big focus for entrepreneurs is carving out the time to design the medium term and long term direction of the company. This should include the path of incrementally expanding from one laser focused niche strategy to the next.

Know how you are going to make money

During the Internet bubble, far too many investors got burned because they never had a solid grasp on how their portfolio companies were going to make money. The company that John Friess's employer was working for – Kozmo.com – was a great example of this.

Despite raising a whopping $250 million, simple math could confirm that the company could never be profitable. The company had sporadic orders, no delivery charge, no minimum purchase, and wafer thin retail margins. Orange puffy jacket wearing "Kozmo runners" often made only three deliveries per hour. Package delivery experts like FedEx and UPS were probably laughing rather than quaking in their boots. The experts knew that the scale of purchasing would need to be many times greater than that required for next day delivery in order to be profitable. People just don't make that many purchases. Moreover, the vast majority of people that live in dense urban areas can get truly instant retail gratification within a couple of blocks of their dwelling.

The moral of this story is simple. If you start a business, then you should know from day one how and when you are going to make money.

Stop planning and start building

Spending time building a massively detailed business plan is more likely to turn you into a 'non-trepreneur" than an entrepreneur. Any plan you build will likely be obsolete within a couple of months, if not weeks. If it is not, then you are operating with inadequate flexibility.

If you know what you are building, how you are going to build it, and have access to enough capital to just get off the ground, then it is time to start building. The entrepreneur's mantra is launch, test, iterate... launch, test, iterate. A shortened form that is easier to remember is 'execute and iterate.' You have to suspend disbelief and accept that the fuel, the landing gear, and the runway, will appear in time for you to safely land the plane.

Sell continuously

Successful entrepreneurs are always selling. They sell to customers. They sell to investors. They sell to employees. Even opportunities without a monetary outcome add another dime to the brand piggy-bank. Finally, as John Friess indicated in his third lesson, entrepreneurs should make sure that every individual within the organization knows how to sell at least on some level.

Recap

Here are the concepts you can immediately (well...) apply to become a successful entrepreneur:

- Find an idea that inspires you, your team, and your customers
- Balance the why, the how, and the what
- Know how you are going to make money
- Stop planning and start building
- Sell continuously

PART FIVE:

YOU (PERSONAL & PROFESSIONAL DEVELOPMENT)

Chapter Twenty Four:
Time Management

As a general manager, the most precious resource you have is time. To excel, you need to upgrade the manner by which you deal with new projects and underlying tasks. The 'Delete, Delegate, Do' framework provides a highly effective approach to time management.

First, delete unessential tasks

Having established a reputation for expert statistical analysis skills, I am frequently called upon to assist others when they hit a brick wall. This means that many of the projects that I engage on are predestined to be grueling and time consuming. So, I have learned that it is critical to carefully review all requests.

In one such project, my company's customer service organization called me into a meeting with an interesting request. They wanted me to develop a complex algorithm to prioritize which clients to proactively contact based on usage of our products, satisfaction scores, and so on. In my early days, I would have jumped immediately at the opportunity to be the hero that solved the unsolvable. In my older, perhaps wiser, and far busier incarnation, I started to probe. My first question, as always, was: 'What is the problem that you are trying to solve?' The service team responded with a worthy goal; they were on a mission to enhance client satisfaction through direct client outreach

Taking a consultative approach, I explored whether there were other ways to achieve this goal. As it turned out, there was ample capacity in the service organization to proactively call every single client in the target population within a reasonable amount of time. Hence, there was no real need to prioritize. The customer service team could initiate their program immediately and I could delete the arduous task of constructing a complex algorithm before I even started. Moreover, by using a consultative approach, I emerged as an even greater hero by suggesting a superior outcome.

Keep in mind, though, that it is neither constructive nor helpful to your reputation and your career to delete tasks lightly. To assess whether or not an action can be deleted, identify whether there is a real problem to solve and determine whether it is large enough to be worth addressing. Many tasks will fail to meet these criteria. If there is a valid problem, explore if there are more efficient approaches that result in equivalent if not better outcomes. In a good number of these cases, you will be able to delete the task.

Next, delegate tasks you can reliably entrust to others

After deleting all unessential tasks, your next step is to delegate all tasks you can reliably entrust to others. To delegate effectively, select individuals that already possess the requisite skills to be successful. You owe it to them to share why the problem is worth solving lest they attempt to delete the task.

Do the rest (and remember to single task)

In the end, you will be left with a set of tasks that can neither be deleted nor delegated. For these projects, I recommend applying the lightest possible prioritization. Tasks should fall into two simple categories. The first is the "Do It Now" category of items that you can and should tackle immediately. Everything else falls into the "Schedule It Now" category.

There is a vast ocean between "Schedule It Now" and "Do It Later" and I choose this language very carefully. The busier you become, the less free time there is on your calendar. I can guarantee that those tasks that are not actively scheduled for completion either will end up not getting done (in which case you should have deleted them to begin with) or will need to be done during precious evenings and weekends. This latter behavior will not be appreciated by your family, your friends, or your doctor.

Perhaps the most important advice I can provide is that you should exclusively single-task. In the words of psychiatrist Richard Hallowell, multitasking is a "mythical activity in which people believe they can perform two or more tasks simultaneously." Though you are no doubt able to walk and chew gum at the same time, actions that engage the thinking brain like processing e-mails, participating in conference calls, and building presentations should be done in isolation. Single tasking will pay dividends in speed and quality, not to mention reputation; you do not want to be the one on the conference call that always says, "Can you please repeat that?"

Recap

The "Delete, Delegate, Do" framework is an invaluable tool for effective time management. Occasionally, you will find a fourth "D", for Delay, inserted between delegating and doing. I strongly recommend against this extra step. If a task needs to be completed and you do not have time to do it immediately, then your best tactic is to actively schedule the time required.

Here are the concepts you can immediately apply to be a proficient time manager:
- First, delete unessential tasks
- Next, delegate tasks you can reliably entrust to others
- Do the rest (and remember to single task)

Chapter Twenty Five: Public Speaking

When I changed jobs from being a semiconductor engineer to an information technology analyst, I realized immediately that success or failure in my future career would rest upon my then undeveloped public speaking ability. More by chance than design, I stumbled upon a local Toastmasters International club. This non-profit educational organization helps members develop their public speaking skills in a zero risk, feedback rich environment. I owe everything I have learned about presenting to this organization and its members. The only way to become a stellar public speaker is to practice, practice, practice. Consequently, the best advice that I can offer is for you to join a local Toastmasters club so that you can apply the detailed tips provided here.

As you develop your public speaking aptitude, focus on improving one presentation skill at a time. In my experience, the most common challenges that neophyte speakers have are eliminating filler words such as "um" or "ah", controlling nervous energy, and figuring out what to do with their arms. If, for example, you are on a mission to eliminate filler words from your speaking, then find a safe environment and focus solely on that for a while. Do not worry about content, style, or any other aspects of delivery. When you reach a sufficient level of competency (remember that mastery is asymptotic), move on to the next critical skill.

Control your environment

Public speaking is a performance that you are giving for your audience. Just as stage directors ensure that everything is ready before the curtain comes up on a play, great presenters take control of their environment. You must arrive early so that you have adequate time to assimilate or modify the technology and physical space.

If you are using technology, leave no stone unturned. Test your microphone. Run through your slides in presentation mode to ensure the computer is functioning and that graphics are displaying as expected. It is easy to fall into complacency. Once, I inserted a graphic for an innocent enough stop sign into a presentation and did not perform a dry run. To my shock and horror, the stop sign began flashing obnoxiously in a presentation before the senior leadership of my company. Fortunately, they had a sense of humor, but I learned that you can never be too careful.

Understanding and even changing your environment is just as important as testing the technology. Regardless of whether or not you can alter your environment, you should take the time to plan how you will use the physical space. For example, if you have the freedom to move around while speaking, you can determine where to stand and which pathways to take. If you can alter the environment, you might choose to reconfigure chairs and tables, add or remove a podium, or reposition a moveable whiteboard.

Arriving early to gain control of the environment will give you confidence that will carry over into your presentation. However, there is yet another compelling benefit. Once you have mastered the technology and the physical space, arriving early gives you a golden opportunity to build rapport with your audience before you speak. By listening carefully, you will create allies and be able to draw their insights and stories into your speech.

Develop your personal speaking style

As you gain comfort with presenting, your personal speaking style will begin to shine through. For most presenters, their speaking style is a magnified version of their day-to-day personality. Though you can develop a presentation persona that is different from who you are, the best advice in speaking is the same advice that applies to courtship – be yourself.

In a corporate environment, the most respected speaking persona is the 'passionate presenter' who radiates confidence and enthusiasm. This style will allow you to shine in most situations including selling your ideas and motivating the troops. There are plenty of good presenters with this style. The great presenters are able to pair passion with sincerity so they rise above being viewed as merely silver tongued. The key is to not let style overwhelm substance.

There are of course other styles besides the 'passionate presenter'. Personas run the gamut from witty to humorous to angry to dramatic. Such styles are rare in the corporate environment since they are outside the norm and can be inappropriate in common situations. For example, while being witty is pleasant, if you use humor excessively then you will not be taken seriously; avoid opening your presentation with a joke unless you are performing in a comedy club. Likewise, it is never appropriate to insult yourself or your audience.

Seasoned speakers know that they, not their slides, are the presenters. They possess the agility to weave stories in such a way that the slides become parenthetical (albeit supportive). One of the tactical ways to make this magic happen is to never expose the guts of the performance. The audience does not care how many hours you spent preparing or that you were up all night. More subtly, you should avoid references to the slides themselves such as "in the next slide, we will see that…" Again, always remember that you, not your props, are the attraction.

Another critical stylistic tip to bear in mind is that you are on stage any time your audience can see you. Your manner of dress, grooming, and comportment should be consistent with your message. In addition to the rapport building that you do before the presentation, your performance includes everything you do from the moment you stand up from your chair to the time you sit down. Walk tall when coming and going, and if the situation warrants, smile liberally.

Regardless of which style you choose, you owe it to your audience to be prepared. Many of those I have coached who are new to public speaking interpret this as a call to fully draft their speech, some even going so far as to read their speeches aloud. Your audience did not come to listen to you read, nor did they come to hear you mechanically deliver your words. They came to be inspired, to learn, to make a personal connection that transforms them in large or small ways. Prepare and rehearse, but do not read your presentation or memorize it. Instead, memorize only your opening and your closing, and simply keep a mental outline of what lies between.

When people finish their prepared remarks, they often let down their guard for the question and answer period. However, it is critical that you develop a style for this portion of your speech as well. You are still very much on stage. When answering questions, you communicate respect to your audience by repeating the question. After you answer, you should seek confirmation by asking "Did I answer your question?" and then looking carefully at the body language of the person that asked the question as well as at that of the rest of the audience.

During a question and answer period, generally strive to maintain the same tone – typically confident and passionate – that you used in your speech. Continuity of tone coupled with repetition and reinforcement of important points will cement your overall message. Note that confidence does not imply that you need to answer every question. You need to know when you do not know. You are a far more credible speaker when you say "Great question. I do not have the answer right now but would be happy to take your contact information during the break so I can get back to you."

A final stylistic point is that you should leave enough time at the end of the question and answer period for a prepared close. This practice reflects utmost professionalism and allows you take back control of the stage. To close, provide a summary of your main points or a call to action.

Architect your content

The key to crafting compelling content is to consider your material from the perspective of your audience: how does it benefit them? Your mission is to determine a single (and I mean single) purpose, key take away, or call to action. This anchor message should be used as the beginning and the ending of your presentation. For example, if I were giving a presentation on speech-craft, I might begin with the following: "At the end of the next ten minutes, you are going to walk away with three valuable techniques that will trans-form your public speaking ability from good to great." That is the kind of beginning that makes most people, except for the most jaded, lean forward in their chairs.

Keep it simple. Simplicity begins with crafting only one purpose, key take away, or call-to-action. As you build a story around that anchor message, stick to a limited number of messages.

Keeping your primary message straightforward and the number and complexity of supporting messages to a minimum is half the battle in ensuring that you get through to your audience. The second half is structuring the content in a way that makes it effortless to process. When you are speaking, even if only for a few minutes, your audience will drift in and out of focusing on you. One moment they fully comprehend the social ramifications of textile bartering in pre-Colonial America and the next moment they are remembering to pick up a gallon of milk from the store on their way home. Regardless of how enthralling the speech or speaker is, unbroken focus cannot be sustained.

There are two excellent ways to deliver content so that your audience will be able to follow along in spite of human deficits in attention. The first approach is to use a structured content framework. The second is to work your content into a story.

Though there are an infinite number of structured content frameworks, the key to using any one of them for delivering content is to expose the framework itself. One of the most effective frameworks is: Tell them what you are going to tell them. Tell them. Then, tell them what you just told them. This structure forces you to employ one of the most effective and sadly underused speaking techniques – repetition.

Another sound structural approach is to use the situation-complication-resolution-next steps framework. The situation lays bare the facts at hand. The complication piece details the set of issues or problems that are in play. In the resolution section, you detail a number of possible solutions and highlight the one that you recommend. Last, next steps provides your audience with an inspiring call to action.

Though it takes more preparation and skill than using a structured framework, telling a story is the single best method to cement your message in the subconscious of your audience. People have a remarkable ability to fill gaps in stories and to apply stories to their personal situations and values. Moreover, stories have layers and layers of meaning that a litany of facts can never convey. One of my favorite quotes of all time is the following: "Tell me a fact and I will learn. Tell me the truth and I will believe. Tell me a story and it will live in my heart forever." Before you think that storytelling is not applicable in a corporate environment, think again. You can inject miniature stories within broader presentations to add truth and impact. Or, you can weave a story of the future of your company or product and inspire your audience to dream with you.

Practice thoughtful slide use and design

With ubiquitous software, printing and display technology, slides have infiltrated human existence. In most developed countries, the indoctrination begins in the classroom for children still in their single digits. By the time people are well into their professional lives, slides become both a primary means of capturing completed work and of sharing messages.

The main problem with slides in the context of public speaking is the irreconcilable tension that exists between using slides as an information repository and using slides for storytelling. Most slides begin their existence as the former integrating tables of data, complex graphics, and most typically page after page of bulleted lists. Most people then take these original slides, clean them up a bit, and use them in a presentation. The slides serve the convenient role of a safety net and the worst offenders simply read bullets off the slide with a few verbal flourishes.

This does not mean that the best presentations eschew slides altogether. The best analogy I can offer is that great presentations are like great movies. There are a few singular movies with no music such as Alfred Hitchcock's "The Birds" and David Lynch's more avant-garde "Eraserhead." Similarly, there are a few exquisite films with no dialogue at all including Sylvain Chomet's "The Triplets of Belleville." However, the vast majority of great movies combine stunning imagery and compelling dialogue with a subtle, emotion-eliciting soundtrack. In a presentation, you are the imagery, your content is the dialogue, and the slides are the background music. Poorly constructed slides can ruin a presentation just as fast as a bad score can ruin a movie.

As you set out to prepare slides that you will use for a public presentation, throw away your information dense research slides, or at least put them on the other side of the room. Grab pen and paper, sticky notes, or a whiteboard, and start to draw out the story you wish to tell. There is no need for you to be a trained graphic designer or artist. Many gifted presenters follow the mantra "say it, then show it." To achieve this, imagine that each slide you draw is the accompanying exclamation point on the part of the story you are sharing.

As you shift from analog to digital, keep your slides nearly as simple as your drawings. Second, make your titles strong enough that they provide the "so-what" in such a way that they alone could tell the story. Third, do not provide handouts before your presentation unless absolutely necessary. At best, your audience will be mildly distracted reading along. At worst, they will scan your entire presentation end to end during the crucial opening minutes of your presentation and then conclude that they have learned everything you have to offer.

Perhaps one in a thousand people that prepare and deliver presentations even have a rudimentary understanding of graphic design. Knowing just a few basic rules governing the use of text and images will give you an incredible edge. (If you run into a snobby graphic designer just remember to say things like "Rules are meant to be broken" and "Helvetica is so jejune.")

The most critical rule of graphic design that applies to slide building is "less is more." Strive for individual slides to be simple and elegant and for the entire deck to form one harmonious whole. For starters, use the minimum possible number of words or directly relevant graphics that you need to get your point across. Again, your voice will be the soundtrack providing additional detail. Minimalism extends to limiting the number of fonts, colors, and images used.

Most designers will employ just a single font in a design. Since many slides have titles or short key headline style messages, your best choice is a variant of Helvetica, including its cousin Ariel. (try to ignore the Helvetica Holy War that has raged for decades in the graphic design community). Every font carries an emotional context and you should strive to match the typeface to your message. For Helvetica, the mood is neutral yet authoritative – hence a good choice for corporate presentations. Nearly every sign you see and company logo you come across is constructed with this font.

If you want or need to use multiple fonts, the best advice is to stay within the same family. Beyond size, fonts vary in thickness (light, regular, and **bold**), as well as other attributes such as *italics*. All of these variations, in addition to sparing use of a different font color, will provide contrast. However, you are bound to run into a rare special circumstance where you need something even more starkly different. In that case, you need to dive just a little into the technical details of fonts.

Helvetica is a sans-serif font, meaning that the ends of the characters do not have little semi-decorative lines. If you wish to mix Helvetica with another family, it is best to do so with a serif font or a script font to make the contrast look intentional and not accidental. While sans-serif fonts like Helvetica are great for headlines, a serif font such as Times New Roman is more commonly used for longer passages of text since the little details help quickly guide the eye. Consequently, if you look closely at most advertisements, you will see Helvetica for titles and Times New Roman for body text. Maybe it is not clever or creative, but it is everywhere because it works and is an excellent choice for the rest of us. The mood for Times New Roman is credible and classic. If you need bold contrast, then you can (again very judiciously) use a script font. I recommend Lucilda Calligraphy which conveys the air of elegant handwriting.

The "less is more" rule also applies to the use of color. Choose a limited palette of at most five colors. To maintain consistency between images, fonts, and backgrounds, an excellent practice is to draw the colors from an image or set of images in the presentation. Many of the most effective palettes are actually monochromic where the color (hue) stays the same, but the lightness/darkness (tone or value) and brightness/dullness (saturation) vary. Alternatively, you can go for subtle but clear contrast with an analogous color scheme which is one in which colors are adjacent on a color wheel. For bold contrast, to be used sparingly, go for complementary colors that sit on opposite sides of the color wheel.

In addition to the colors contained in fonts and images, you should also be thoughtful about the colors used in slide backgrounds and foreground. As a general rule, use cool colors such as blue, green, or silver for backgrounds and warm colors like red, yellow, and orange for foregrounds. Neutral colors like black and white may also be suitable for backgrounds.

In addition to the "less is more" philosophy, another set of principles worth internalizing regards attentive placement of text and images. Again, this is the stuff of design community battles, but the basics rule in the end, via the Rule of Thirds, to be exact. Just divide a slide into a three-by-three grid of nine equal sized boxes, using this grid to align both text and images. It is perfectly acceptable and accepted for elements to span multiple boxes but do so with awareness and intention. For example, imagine that you consumed an entire slide with a single outdoor photograph. In that case, you would align the horizon with one of the two horizontal grid lines. If the sky is dull, align it with the top one. If dramatic, then align the horizon with the bottom grid line. Additionally, the grid is your guide to where the focal points are on the slide. There are five of them. The first four are at the intersections of the grid lines and make excellent places to place an image. The fifth one is more subtle and is at the visual center of the slide just up and to the right of true center.

As for using images, the sky is the limit. Just remember to use only images that are relevant to the message. Avoid pictures that provide mere decoration, including most generic clipart. Oh, and one more helpful tip. Where possible, consider bleeding images off the page; this stimulates people to use their imagination to compete the picture.

Manage your physical delivery

When I first started to develop my public speaking ability, my greatest weakness was that I did not know what to do with my hands. When I consulted reference materials, I either heard useless generalizations (do what comes naturally) or read lists of what not to do. I yearned for something or someone to tell me what ideal physical delivery looks like.

To be comfortable with what do with your arms, just do what you do when you are having a standing conversation with somebody you trust. When people speak to one another, their rest position is to have their hands comfortably down at their sides. This is the most effective base position in public speaking. Next, you want to make natural gestures above the waist, but below the neck. For about half the population, hand gestures are a natural part of the way they converse. If you fit into that group, just keep doing what you are doing. If you are in the other half like me, then you are going to have to force yourself to make hand gestures lest you stand uncomfortably fixed like a soldier. It is going to feel awkward initially, but I promise your discomfort will disappear in no time. The only difference between what you do with your arms in normal conversation versus what you do in public speaking is that you should make your hand gestures somewhat larger. The bigger your audience, the more dramatic your gestures need to be for people to see them.

Rather than hands down comfortably at their sides with elbows slight bent, many people believe that the correct base position is to keep their hands above the waist at all times. Some people put their hands together, some people keep them apart. You can most certainly be a good speaker if you do this, but you will not be great. Imagine walking around all day, every day like this. It would be neither comfortable nor confident. Remember, you would never have a conversation with a person whom you care about with your hands up the entire time, because it creates a barrier. Even at a distance, you will be creating the same barrier with your audience.

Now that I have shared with you what you should do with your arms while speaking, it is worth knowing what not to do. Do not hold your hands in any of the following positions:
* Fig leaf: Holding your arms down but with your hands coupled in front suggests that you are timid.
* Pockets: Hands in pockets makes you appear passive or disinterested.
* Parade rest: Holding your arms down but with your hands coupled in back suggests that you are hiding something.
* Hips: Hands on hips makes you appear defiant.
* Crossed arms: Crossing your arms is a negative, challenging position.

Effective use of your arms is just one component of physical delivery. Another is transmitting positive body language. For starters, you should shower your audience with a genuine smile. Smiles not only communicate calm confidence but also build trust between you and your audience. Though there are many aspects to positive body language, the most important factor beyond your smile is your ability to keep your body square and balanced. Face your audience, keep your shoulders square, and plant your feet on the floor shoulder width apart.

Once you master your smile and your stance, you must develop your eye-contact skills. The key to being expert at eye-contact is to make direct eye contact with specific individuals in the audience. Rather than scanning the audience (or worse, the ceiling or the floor), aim to make direct eye-contact with one person at a time, with that contact lasting the duration of a thought. This literally means holding eye contact for a minimum of a dozen or so seconds while you make it through a sentence or two.

Once you have mastered the physical delivery skills of hand gestures and body language, you can transform yourself into a true professional through the use of effective movement. Your goal is to make your movement fluid and natural while still retaining discipline. Making this concrete, I recommend that you move on transitions. Remain in one spot with your body square to your audience as you make a point. Then pause and move. Once you have stopped, begin speaking again. Rather than being awkward, this pause gives your audience time to process your last point and to prepare for your next one. Of course there are times when you may wish to travel a longer distance. In those instances, you can speak while moving. However, when you get to your new position make sure to stop and square up your body so that you do not appear to be wandering or pacing.

Master your verbal delivery

To become an excellent public speaker, you must master your verbal delivery. Fortunately, you have fertile opportunities to practice, as public speaking is generally an amplified version of your everyday conversations. This is of course a double edged sword. The imperfections that exist in your regular speech will be magnified during presentations. However, with a small amount of practice you can transform your verbal delivery both on and off stage.

If you are like most people, then your speech has become infected with filler words. People use filler words because they are uncomfortable with silence. The most common are "um" and "ah", but the more evolved have masked these with "so", "actually" and even the occasional lip smack. More insidious, though in the same category, are the words and phrases "like", "you know", "sort of" and "kind of" since they express uncertainty, not to mention immaturity, in what you are saying.

Fortunately, the cure for using filler words is simple. Just pause. The pause not only replaces filler words, but also gives you an aura of self-control. A brief silence provides time to collect and structure your next thoughts. Beyond the personal benefits, the pause gives your audience the time they need to process what you are saying. Longer pauses add dramatic emphasis like a subtle yet powerful exclamation point. They grab your audience's attention. The pause is a gift that keeps giving.

One you have eliminated most filler words by mastering the art of the pause, you must add vocal variety to make your speech interesting. Start by modulating your volume. If you speak softer, you will actually cause people to lean forward in their seats and take notice. If louder, then you command attention. Either way, take full, deep breaths and project so that people in the last row can hear you. Next vary the speed. For example, you can gradually increase the speed and shorten sentences to add excitement. Though some dramatic speakers vary pitch (high and low) and cadence (rhythmic rise and fall of voice inflection), these vocal traits can come across as artificial in a corporate setting.

Your verbal delivery extends beyond speech mechanics into the words that you use. To enhance your audience's interest, you should make liberal use of vivid, descriptive, sensory detail. Sights, sounds, and smells are the easiest to incorporate. In some situations, you may even be able to weave in taste and touch. The small penalty you pay in being verbose is more than made up for by the impact you have of allowing your audience to form a mental picture.

Recap

Here are the concepts you can immediately apply to become a polished public speaker:
- Control your environment
- Develop your personal speaking style
- Architect your content
- Practice thoughtful slide use and design
- Manage your physical delivery
- Master your verbal delivery

Chapter Twenty Six: Storytelling

As our culture has evolved from an oral tradition to a digital one, great story-tellers have become rare and highly valued. Though the scarcity of experts will make finding a mentor difficult, you can develop excellent storytelling abilities on your own.

As with any learned skill, you must practice every day to move toward mastery. Fortunately, you can make storytelling a habit by working narratives into every day conversation. A story can be as simple as an anecdote or as expansive as a case study. One excellent way to introduce storytelling into your life is to set a goal to make one 'non-smiler' smile each day.

Becoming an accomplished storyteller will provide enormous personal and pro-fessional benefits. On a personal level, talented storytellers are the life of the party. In professional settings, you will rapidly find that people who excel at spinning yarns are far more effective in communicating ideas and motivating others to action.

Find, repeat, and refine your stories

For blossoming storytellers, the most daunting task is discovering stories to begin with. How often have you heard someone recount an amazing tale and then said to yourself 'wow, if my life were only that interesting, then I could tell great stories too.' I am here to tell you that your life is that interesting. Any situation in which you felt inspired, enraged, or even embarrassed is story fod-der. In fact, any event or interaction that ignited an emotional response is fair game. The rest is up to you.

With rare exception, the most compelling narratives are about your personal experiences. One of my favorite modern storytellers, David Sedaris, exempli-fies the art of transforming the everyday into the absurd. For example, take the time Mr. Sedaris summoned a plumber to his apartment in Paris. Instead of saying merely that he needed the tradesman to fix a commode that would not stop running, he describes how he used broken French to say 'My toilet... she cries much of the time.'

Most of us spend our days moving hurriedly from place to place without deeply paying attention to what is happening all around us. We eat breakfast while thinking about our drive to work. We drive to work while thinking about our ten-o-clock meeting. We sit in our meeting while pondering what we will eat for lunch. To be an effective tale weaver, you must closely observe the people and the environment that surround you in the here and now. Buddhists refer to that state of being as mindfulness. Use all of your senses so that you can incorporate what you see, hear, smell, touch, taste, think, and feel into your narrative.

When you find a solid story, or better yet several of them, refine them through repetition. Polish your ability to recount individual tales and the aura of skilled storytelling will develop around you. Great stories start out as good stories but are gradually enhanced through continual pruning and editing until they become legendary.

Progress from characters to conflict to conclusion

There are innumerable ways to structure plot. However, you will never go wrong with the tried and true approach of starting with characters, putting them in conflict, and then providing a conclusion; This is the situation-complication-resolution recast in another form.

Authentic characters, with all of their warts and complexity, are the basis for any riveting story. By identifying with specific character traits, listeners imagine themselves or people they care about as the protagonists. To help your audience form this bond, introduce your characters at the beginning of your story with highly descriptive language. Though human beings are the most effective characters for this purpose, you can easily substitute companies, animals, settings, or whatever suits your purpose. In order to set the stage for the coming conflict, make sure to clearly communicate the needs and desires of your characters.

By putting obstacles between your characters and their needs, you inject conflict in a way that triggers your audience's sense of empathy and their desire to problem solve. Presenting a single obstacle can be highly effective. Keeping things simple is indeed the best approach when you have limited time to convey a story. However, your best strategy is to build progressively more intense barriers for your characters to overcome, all the while keeping the carrot just in front of their noses. This will fuel intensity and suspense.

Every story should have either a positive or negative ending. (Yes, a cliffhanger is the third option, but that is best saved for movies with planned sequels.) Stories with positive endings are highly effective for inspiration. They make people say and believe, 'I can do that.' In contrast, cautionary tales are more effective for teaching. Since pleasure is a more powerful long term motivation than pain, I recommend telling stories with positive endings the vast majority of the time.

The time to pull out the calamity tale is when you are trying to instill the virtues of safety to audiences that work in dangerous professions like construction or law enforcement. Nothing says "pay attention" like 'listen, or you might be the next one to die in a careless, preventable accident.' If you do tell a story that ends in disaster, spend time at the end exploring ways that the characters could have avoided their fate.

Connect with the deep needs of your listeners

For your stories to have lasting impact, you must strive to connect with listeners on one or more of the four chords of emotional resonance. In doing so, you provide your audience with nourishment on their journey to self-actualization.

The first chord to strike is the fundamental human need for love and belonging. Everyone wants to be proud of their lives. They want to feel that they are important, known, and understood. In some professions, like teaching and healthcare, people have ample opportunities to connect their work to the positive impact they have on individuals and the world at large. However, in most professions, employees are many steps removed from that impact. As a storyteller, you have an opportunity to help connect people to an inspiring noble purpose.

The second chord to play is an appeal to desire and self-interest. Though less dignified than love and belonging, this emotional facet is equally powerful. By way of example, an appeal to self-interest is highly effective in situations where you are motivating people to confront a threat to job security or life and limb.

The third chord to play is inspiring self-development. Human beings are wired to be curious about the world so that they can grow personally and professionally. Through their indirect nature, stories allow people to think for themselves in a way that builds new skills faster than by absorbing facts. A story about the way someone rose from mail room clerk to chief executive officer is far more effective than a bulleted checklist of leadership skills.

The fourth chord to strike is that of providing hope. This is achieved with stories that paint a promising tomorrow that is both reachable and worth the effort.

The four chords are so powerful because they provide a connection between your message or call to action and the fundamental needs that your audience already feels are important.

Establish trust with your audience

To accept you as a storyteller and, more importantly, your message, an audience must trust you. Because you will often be an unknown quantity, you must weave the threads of trust directly into your stories.

Openness builds trust instantly. When you are selling an idea or motivating action, your audience will begin listening with a healthy dose of skepticism. To bring down their defenses, you should strive to give evidence of what is in it for you before you share what is in it for them. Your motives must be honest, genuine, and pure. An intelligent audience will rapidly see through smoke and mirrors. In addition, you exude openness when you use language, gestures, tone, and body language that is congruent and genuine.

Another way to establish trust is by demonstrating your credibility. If you are telling a story to inspire people to replace energy inefficient lighting with greener options, then you are swimming upstream if your family of three lives in a six thousand square foot home with an Olympic sized swimming pool and finely manicured grounds. You must show that you walk the walk and that you care.

A final way to establish trust is by showing respect for your audience. Some speakers make the mistake of expounding at length on their pedigree, believing this lends gravitas. If you have been given a chance to speak, you have already been accepted as an expert. Your objective is to highlight how smart your listeners are, not on how accomplished you are. Though it is safe to challenge conventional wisdom, never challenge your listeners by attempting to prove them wrong.

Allow subtlety to triumph

The mark of a great story is that it allows the listener to discover layer upon layer of wisdom through interpretation. This subtlety lies in not being overtly outcome focused. To enable the listener to peel the onion, you must make your stories rich in personal, emotional content as well as vivid sensory detail.

Stories need not be objective. In fact, the most compelling stories are told from a subjective point of view. You need your emotions to shine through and that can only be achieved if you express your most strongly held beliefs. An interesting twist on this theme is to tell a story sequentially from multiple, distinct points of view.

Above all, you will be far more successful with upbeat stories than with negative ones, even in an environment of disillusionment; if applicable, first acknowledge what is wrong, but then move toward positive outcomes. People crave speakers and stories that are authentic, yes, but also passionate and fun.

Recap

Here are the concepts you can immediately apply to become a thought-provoking storyteller:
* Find, repeat, and refine your stories
* Progress from characters to conflict to conclusion
* Connect with the deep needs of your listeners
* Establish trust with your audience
* Allow subtlety to triumph

Chapter Twenty Seven:
Body Language

To advance your personal relationships and professional career, study body language. After covering a set of guiding principles, I will take you through reading body language from head to toe.

Develop personal body language awareness and alter bad habits

On a personal level, you should not struggle to control your own body language. That is a lost cause, since most behaviors come from parts of the brain over which you have little or no control. Moreover, you are more likely to be seen as manipulative rather than wise if you manufacture body language.

Instead, you should strive to do two things. The first is to develop body language awareness. This means understanding the resonance between what you are thinking and how you are expressing your feelings. The second is to alter habits that you have that unintentionally communicate negative body language. The classic example is people that have developed a habit of crossing their arms for reasons of comfort.

Understand that body language reveals stress and comfort, not truth and lies

There is a common fallacy that having the ability to read body language makes you into a human lie detector. Though not entirely incorrect, the accurate assessment is that the ability to read body language makes you a human mood ring. Specifically, body language reveals the absence or presence of stress and discomfort.

Find baseline behaviors and look for clusters of dissonance

In most situations where you are going to be actively reading body language, the person you are observing will be in an environment with an elevated level of pressure or excitement. In personal settings, this might be a first date or a heated argument. In professional ones, this might be a negotiation or a critical meeting. Moreover, from day to day, people may be in a good or a bad mood due to events that have nothing to do with your immediate interaction. Consequently, you should strive to establish a set of baseline behaviors that are specific to both the person and to the situation. Since people aim to be at ease, you can assume that the baseline is the comfortable state.

Once you have determined the set of baseline behaviors, your job is to detect changes that show evidence of stress. If someone who ordinarily crosses their arms braces them on their chair, you have one piece of evidence. As in any investigation, one piece of evidence alone does not make the case. Hence, to be great at reading body language, you need to find clusters of behaviors. Remember that although many clusters are purely physical, you should also look for dissonance between words and behaviors. A good example is when people shake their head "no" or look down when they say "yes." One of my all-time favorites is discord in words such as when a person says "No, I agree with you."

Read the head and neck

Body language begins with the very top of the head. When people touch their own hair, they are either subconsciously preening themselves or trying to sooth themselves. The preening angle, particularly by women, is why hair touching is considered flirtatious in social situations. It subtly communicates that a person is available and willing to relax some degree of control. In contrast to the social interpretation, people in more stressful circumstances touch their hair to capture a soothing tactile response and release negative energy. Individuals that develop a hair touching habit have become addicted in large and small ways to this comfort.

Progressing to the forehead, signs of stress include furrowing the forehead by contracting facial muscles as well as rubbing one's forehead. The interpretation of a furrowed forehead ranges from confusion to outright disagreement. From the situation itself and clusters of other behaviors, you will learn to know where in that spectrum the person lies. Rubbing one's forehead stimulates blood flow to the brain. Again, the meaning can vary from mere tiredness to true stress.

The eyes are where most people look for body language. Stress is evidenced by variation from the baseline in squinting, closing, shielding, averting, and blinking. With respect to blinking, for example, you may detect either a faster than normal or slower than normal blink rate. The completely false conventional wisdom is that people break eye contact when they are lying. Since virtually everyone believes this is true, you are wise, actually, to look for abnormally direct eye contact when someone is uncomfortable and possibly lying. This preternaturally direct gaze is often coupled with restricted motion because it takes everything a person has to maintain eye contact with lying. Lest you believe you can control this yourself, think again. If you are lying, then odds are you will either have too little or too much eye contact and there is nothing you can do about it. A better approach is never to lie in the first place. On a positive note, high arched eyebrows and "flashbulb" eyes communicate genuine interest.

There are multiple signs of stress in the cheeks. The more obvious include rubbing the inside of the cheeks with the tongue or biting. Since many people have an oral fixation of one kind or another, these behaviors are more often than not simply baseline habits that provide little useful information.

The mouth is one of the most expressive parts of the body. The oral fixation that afflicts the tongue also afflicts the mouth so be careful to not over-interpret the meaning of lip and nail biting. However, pursing the lips is a telltale sign of discomfort. Additionally, mechanisms that increase the supply of oxygen to the blood are signs of stress. These include slow exhales as well as excessive yawning. Of course, the mouth has the ability to display one of the most positive behaviors – the smile. Unlike a fake grin or smirk, a genuine smile includes mouth corners turned up and "crow's feet" emanating from the eyes.

Your examination of body language in the head ends with the chin and neck. When people are stressed, they often tilt their head forward, forcing their chin down. This often subconscious action protects the vital arteries in the neck. This protection instinct also is sometimes coupled with a soothing instinct of gently stroking the front or back of one's neck.

Read the upper torso and arms

The majority of stress revealing behaviors in the upper body involve the entire upper torso. All of the relevant expressions of body language link to a preprogrammed need to protect the internal organs from harm. The offending deeds include:

- Turning one's torso away from the other person
- Self-administering a body hug
- Hunching over or bowing (which are viewed as submissive)
- Covering the body with an object such as a pillow or a purse

Consider next the shoulders. When someone is stressed, particularly if they are afraid, you may see their shoulders elevated slightly upward toward their ears. Another interesting tip is what people do with their shoulders when they say "no." Imagine that you are in a negotiation or other situation in which you are asking a person to do something. If they say "no" with a half shoulder shrug, then there is a good chance their refusal is weak. A strong refusal is accompanied by a full shoulder shrug.

Behaviors in the arms and hands are typically intertwined. A confident, comfortable person (possibly making a territorial display) may interlace his or her hands behind the head or spread his or her arms out over adjacent chairs. A more nervous person may touch jewelry or clothing and wring their hands. If a person is aware of his or her behavior, the individual may move to hide discomfort by hiding their hands either in pockets or under thighs.

Here are two final tips on the hands, dealing with the palms and the thumbs. A display of the palms is simultaneously a show of openness and supplication. To that end, if somebody is asking you to do something with palms up, you can let down your guard a little. Though you should only use this technique for good rather than for evil, you can use this method consciously, and in all good conscience, when you are making a request. As for the thumbs, if you have ever injured these fingers, then you know how important they are. Opposable thumbs give humans and precious few other species the gift of fine motor skills. Consequently, people are reflecting comfort when they show their thumbs. Examples include flashing a thumbs-up gesture or having one's hands in one's pockets with the thumbs sticking out.

Read the lower torso

You may be surprised to learn that the lower torso reveals more behavioral information per square inch than any other part of the body. The generally acceptable biological reason for this is that the legs and feet are the farthest parts of the body from the brain. As a result, movement and positioning of the lower torso is the last thing people are able to control. Though most people are oblivious of this fact, criminal investigators are well aware. The best interviewers position themselves in full view of a suspect's lower torso, going so far as to remove tables completely from the equation.

From thighs to knees to feet, the catalog of stress signaling behaviors in the lower torso include:
* Legs directed away from another person
* Rubbing the thighs
* Hands braced on the knees
* Feet locked behind chairs
* Feet positioned toward the exit or in a "starter position" (for a rapid escape)
* Feet close together (viewed as submissive due to the inability to move quickly)
* Feet jiggling or kicking

The last one, jiggling feet, is probably the one that requires the most confirmation from clusters of other behaviors. In a positive situation, these can easily be a sign of happy feet.

Just as with all other parts of the body, there are manifestations of positive body language in the lower torso beginning with opposites of the behavior described above. A fun additional one is noticing which way people cross their legs. In particular, individuals tend to cross their legs with their raised foot in the direction of the person they favor. Finally, the leg splay joins the arm splay as a sign of comfortable, albeit territorial, body language.

Recap

Here are the concepts you can immediately apply to become adroit at reading body language:

- Develop personal body language awareness and alter bad habits
- Understand that body language reveals stress and comfort, not truth and lies
- Find baseline behaviors and look for clusters of dissonance
- Read the head and neck
- Read the upper torso and arms
- Read the lower torso

Chapter Twenty Eight: Charisma

When I applied to the Booth School of Business at the University of Chicago, I was required to subject myself to a three-hundred sixty degree evaluation by my peers, friends, and superiors. Most people either elaborated on my budding strengths or shared innocuous observations. However, one person dared to share more critical feedback, writing "you are an intelligent, analytical person but need to develop poise to advance your future career." Those words immediately dealt a large blow to my self-confidence. I knew what the word poise meant, but as she had accurately observed I did not know the first thing about exhibiting it.

Over time, I became more and more obsessed with the concept of poise. I quickly intuited that poise is not only physical composure but also social and emotional composure. However, my real breakthrough came when I realized that poise is a precursor to rapport and that rapport is the precursor of charm. Several years of further introspection revealed that charm plus genuine persuasion equals charisma, the ultimate tool of influence.

The suggestions which follow will help you build charisma. To accelerate your journey, remember that charisma is a connection that you make one individual at a time. It is also a power to be used only ethically and sincerely.

Mirror the other person

If you observe close friends and family, you will notice that they have a tendency to mirror each other in a multitude of ways spanning verbal and non-verbal communication. Because of this, mimicry is associated with likeability and trust. To rapidly build rapport with others, you should consciously but subtly do the same.

At least half of the information that people exchange during a conversation is non-verbal. You can begin to mirror a person's body language in understated ways. For example, if they have their weight shifted on one leg, then you can do the same. In general, it is best to mirror positive body language, though the principle works with negative body language as well. For example, suppose another individual has their arms crossed not out of comfort but out of disagreement. Once you have synchronized your body language to theirs, you can lead them delicately to relax their arms into a less confrontational position.

Both words and vocal style make up verbal communication. When mirroring another person, you can start by adopting their volume, speed, and tone. Next, align your word selection. The sometimes maligned though generally useful field of neuro-linguistic programming (NLP) provides some guidance here. NLP teaches that people reveal through their word choice the dominant manner in which they process information. For example, visual people might use words like "I see what you are saying..." Auditory people say "I hear what you are saying..." Finally, kinesthetic people use either emotional or tactile words such as "I sense you are right."

Employ tools of influence

In his groundbreaking book "Influence: The Psychology of Persuasion", Professor Robert Cialdini of Arizona State University detailed six methods of influence. Knowing these will help you to exert ethical influence and to defend against manipulation.

- Reciprocity: This concept taps into the human need to repay a favor. To exercise it, you must give something away in order to create a tacit obligation.
- Scarcity: This concept plays to desire. To exercise it, you should be forthright in sharing when you possess something that is rare. If your product or service is not hard to come by and you hold it out to be so, then people will see through the subterfuge and view you as manipulative.
- Authority: This concept draws on social norms of respect. To exercise it, project yourself as an expert by sharing compelling and legitimate evidence.
- Escalation: This concept taps into people's wish to appear consistent in their actions. To exercise it, begin by securing a small commitment and build from there. Despite its power, this one is generally the most manipulative and should be used sparingly, if at all.

- Conformity: This concept leverages the human need to fit in. To exercise it, provide testimonials by independent third parties about the value of your product or service.
- Liking: This concept ties to people's tendency to trust people they like. To exercise it, develop positive relationships and find common interests.

Make the other person know that you sincerely care about him or her

While concepts like reciprocity and escalation represent the more aggressive tools of influence, the principle of liking exemplifies a softer side. Genuinely caring about other people is the essence of charm. In short, people like and trust people that like and trust them. Because this is so important, it bears expanding upon here at some length.

To grasp the power of instant rapport, I encourage you to conduct an easy social experiment. As you walk down the street, smile and make eye contact with others as you pass them. Nine times out of ten, you will see their face light up and return the warmth. Often, the other person will scan your face wondering 'Do I know you from somewhere?' You will also elicit the occasional audible greeting. Remember that there is a huge difference between a genuine smile versus a grin or a smirk. With the latter, only the mouth muscles move. You should also conduct the dark side of the experiment by making eye contact accompanied by a neutral or scowling expression. Most of the time, others will rapidly avert their eyes so that they do not absorb any of your bad karma.

Once, after receiving a promotion, I sought advice from one of my new peers. He recommended that I tone down the volume and frequency of my ubiquitous smile. His belief was that people only take serious people seriously. Nonsense. The power of smiling and eye contact is magnified in the business environment where you have recurring interactions with people. Why? Just ask yourself whom you would rather be around - someone that radiates warmth and happiness or the opposite?

Academic researchers have long known that tactile stimulation, or simply touch, is closely associated with liking. For instance, in 1985, Stanley Jones and Elaine Yarbrough went so far as to study and catalog twelve distinct meanings of physical contact including appreciation, affection, and friendship. The lesson is that appropriate, casual touches, for example to the shoulder or elbow, help build affinity.

Rapport building techniques are more powerful in combination as researchers Jacob Hornik and Shmuel Ellis discovered in 1988. Hornik and Ellis sent graduate students to a suburban Chicago shopping mall to ensnare passersby to participate in a marketing survey. They discovered that, on average, interviewers who made eye contact and a casual touch got 76.4% of people to take part in the survey. Shoppers greeted without these pleasantries only consented 53.4% of the time.

Before you get too taken with this approach, note that gender matters. Though the overall response rate was 65.3%, there were extremes depending on the gender combinations of the interviewers and the shoppers. When a female interviewer touched and made eye contact with male shoppers, the willingness to participate in the survey was a stunning 91.6%. In contrast, when a male interviewer applied the same techniques to female shoppers, the response rate fell to a paltry 55.6%. Lest you conclude that men should avoid appropriate touch to establish trust, consider that male interviewers that approached female shoppers without eye contact or touching only garnered a 47.2% response rate. The touch and gaze combination works to build rapport; it simply works better for women than for men.

To prove that you care about someone, actively listen to what that person has to say. *Sincere interest is interesting.* Great Adept listeners go about their art in a particular way. First, they listen with every fiber of their being including their ears, their eyes, and their body. They listen as if the person they are conversing with is the only other individual in the world. Great listeners ignore every form of distraction including technology such as phones, computers, and watches. Second, they think exclusively about what the other person is saying. Finally, they are ready to speak. Rather than holding a separate, parallel conversation, expert listeners respond constructively to what the other person is saying.

There are few words more pleasant to the ear than one's own name. Hence, to build trust, you should know and address other people by name. As with every recommendation for building rapport, this too must be done with sincerity and subtlety. People like to hear you use their name because it makes them feel known and respected. It shows you felt they were important enough to take the time to commit them to memory. However, avoid using someone's name excessively during a conversation. This behavior, associated with overly-slick salespeople, comes off as purely calculating.

When it comes to building rapport, opposites do not attract. People are drawn to others that look and think like them. Hence, to establish trust, you should strive to identify and highlight similarities. Similarities come in all flavors including physical (ethnicity, height, etc.), situational (alma mater, job function, etc.), and intellectual (hobbies, movies, etc.) Even if you struggle to discover similarities such as these, you can always find areas of agreement in your current conversation.

Just as the conventional wisdom that 'opposites attract' is completely off base when it comes to rapport building, so too is the belief that 'familiarity breeds contempt.' That could not be farther from the truth. The greater the number of interactions that you have with someone, the more likely they are to trust you.

Another important element of being charismatic is showing that you are human. One part of this is exposing your natural sense of humor. People are drawn to others that are witty and light-hearted. The combination of passion and light-heartedness is magical, albeit difficult to achieve. Remember not to take things too far though. Excessive humor, and especially sarcasm, will not win you any points. A second part of showing that you are human is revealing vulnerability through *gradual* emotional self-disclosure. People may respect emotional autom-atons, but they will not follow them. Instead, individuals connect with leaders that have faced and risen above adversity. That way, they have the confidence that you will guide the way in good times and in bad.

Go the extra mile

To be charming, you must go the extra mile to show appreciation for oth-ers. This is one of those obvious rules that everybody knows but to which few adhere. Though better than nothing, a simple "thank you" is not enough. A charming show of appreciation combines sincere gratitude with specific acknowledgement of the effort a person provided as well as what their actions meant to you. For example, imagine that you have asked a colleague to interview candidates for a position that you are filling. A proper show of appreciation is "Thank you for spending twelve hours interviewing candidates for my open position. Your input on Mary's communication skills was instrumental in my decision to hire her."

Sincere, specific appreciation is table stakes. To take your charm to the next level, express your gratitude in ways that demonstrate that you took the time to truly care. You will stand out from the crowd if you employ old world courtesies like hand written thank you notes and relevant gifts. You no doubt receive hundreds of emails every day, but when was the last time you received a genuine handwritten letter? In order to give a relevant gift, you must have purposefully had a social conversation to deeply understand an individual's personal interests. Gift cards and cash are nice but not charming. If you find out someone loves books, probe deeper to see if they like fiction or non-fiction. If non-fiction, then do they enjoy biography, history, business motivation?

The true masters are consistently and continuously charming. To reach that ideal, you must strive to anticipate and proactively address the needs and concerns of others. Concentrate on actions that touch emotional factors such as hope, ambition, desire, and the need to feel important. In the ultimate state of social resonance, you become one with the other person so that your wants and needs are completely aligned.

Follow your own path

Making the other person know that you care and going the extra mile will elevate you from simply building rapport to being charming. If you stop there, then you will have gained the benefits that accrue to a social chameleon. However, to elevate charm to charisma, you must know and express your distinct personality, convictions, and values. Those elements combine to make your personal brand. Follow your own path with audacious passion and with no fear of failure. Express who you are with infectious enthusiasm. Share your vision one person at a time and one moment at a time.

Recap

Here are the concepts you can immediately apply to develop charisma:

- Mirror the other person
- Employ tools of influence
- Make the other person know that you sincerely care about them
- Go the extra mile
- Follow your own path

Chapter Twenty Nine:
Happiness and Meaning

At present, there are nearly fifteen thousand books in print exploring happiness. As if that were not enough, there are another 65 million web pages on the subject. This banquet reveals two things. First, everybody wants to be happy. Second, mankind has yet to crack the code on what guarantees happiness.

As far as I can tell, the singular pursuit of happiness is a destructive behavior in itself. Most human emotions exist in contrasting pairs. Happiness and sadness, contentment and anger, love and hate. If we managed to completely eliminate everything negative, then we could never truly experience ecstasy. Happiness is something that is experienced, not pursued, as you live your life fully mindful of each moment.

You can create a mindset and an environment that will allow you to capture the moments of happiness as they arise. Here is an approach.

Today and every day, find meaning and joy in large and small things

People appreciate what they have and resent what they do not. However, remind yourself to be grateful both for what you do have as well as for what you do not. This allows you to shift your mindset from the negative to the positive. For example, if you live in a small, one-bedroom home, you might waste your days resenting the fact that you do not reside in a mansion. Instead, you would be much better off focusing on the gift you have been given of not being homeless.

There is an excellent Jewish folk take that drives this point home. A poor farmer along with his wife and an army of children and relatives are crammed together in a one room shack. When he goes to his Rabbi to express his misery and seek advice, the farmer is instructed by the sage to bring a chicken into the house. Of course, this only makes things worse. The man returns to the Rabbi who tells him to also bring in the family goat. And so it goes day after day, animal on top of animal, until the living conditions become truly insufferable. At last, the Rabbi tells the farmer to remove all of the animals. In the end, the man learns to appreciate the relative space and quiet that he had to begin with.

In addition to finding joy in what is not, you should strive to perceive the hidden potential in all things. Buddhists have a term – emptiness – that encapsulates this principle. Emptiness highlights that nothing has an inherent positive or negative quality. More concretely, people assign qualities to tangibles and intangibles based on perception and interpretation. Take the feeling one has when lying down in a tranquil, flower filled meadow. For many, this represents the peak of relaxation. For the extreme allergy sufferer, it might be the incarnation of hell on earth. Even in sorrow, there can be joy. Consider the loss of a spouse after fifty years of close companionship. The survivor can dwell on his or her grief or appreciate that the deceased loved one did not have to suffer the loneliness of being the last to go.

All too often, people cannot experience happiness because they are caught up either in the pain of the past or the promise of the future. Again, Buddhists come to the rescue with the principle of mindfulness. This concept teaches us to be fully engaged in the present. Right now, you are just reading (and hopefully enjoying) a book. Spending time thinking about how you got here and where you are going is not going to make you happy.

Searching for one true meaning of life is another major barrier to experiencing happiness. Though a long range meaning to your life may exist, it may or may not reveal itself – and if it does, will do so only at the end. Rather than a being source of stress, the quest to find meaning is a primary motivational force. Embrace the tension this striving creates as necessary for mental health. To free yourself from the tyranny of searching for a single purpose, ask not "What is the meaning of life?" but rather "What *are* the *meanings* in life?" Meanings differ from person to person, from day to day, and from hour to hour. According to existential psychologist and World War II concentration camp survivor Victor Frankl, meanings are found in three areas. First, meanings exist in the work you do. Second, meanings exist in your relationships – especially with the people whom you love. Third, meanings exist in the positive "why" behind unavoidable suffering. For example, a mother dies in childbirth so that her daughter can survive. Finally, before you get yourself all twisted around, you must accept that meaning does not exist in every task, relationship, and situation. Sometimes, you just have to relax and smell the roses.

Today and every day, enjoy and show appreciation for your friends, family, and fellow human beings

Taking the time to show appreciation for others has both selfless and selfish benefits. On the selfless side, your gift of gratitude makes other people feel better about themselves and their value in the world. On the selfish side, every show of appreciation that you provide is another seed you have sown. Some seeds will shrivel. Others will thrive. The more you plant, the greater the chance that you will reap rewards in the future. Remember that appreciation comes not only through actions and words, but also from thoughts.

One of the most compelling though often overlooked ways to show appreciation is bringing other people together. Go the extra mile by giving them ideas and helping them to succeed.

Today and every day, follow your dreams and true purpose

What things would you consider worth doing today if it were your last? Take the time to answer that question to set yourself on the right path. As you proceed, you will need to arm yourself with defenses against self-doubt so that you can continue taking calculated risks.

Remember that the journey is the reward. Stated from another perspective, where you are going is here. Limit unrealistic expectations of yourself and instead take the time to appreciate everything that you have done so far. You are not alone in wondering "How did I get here and when are they going to see that I am a fraud?" Yet, know, truly know, that trying and staying in the game are what matters.

To be able to follow your dreams, you must live for self-recognition, not the recognition of others. In the end, success is based on the quality of what you do and who you are as a human being.

Limit your expectations about the behavior of others

Learning to abandon expectations of yourself while you are on a journey in pursuit of your dreams is only half the battle. The other half is releasing expectations about the behavior of others. If you have ever said to yourself, "I cannot believe that Jane did that!", then you are guilty as charged.

Every individual has a dynamic set of behaviors. Rather than become fixated by someone else in the short term or, worse still, the long term, accept that you simply may not understand their motivations. Generally people act in an internally consistent manner and though often selfish are rarely malicious. Most of the time, the song is simply not about you.

Recap

Here are the concepts you can immediately apply to create a mindset and an environment that will allow you to capture the moments of happiness as they arise:

- Today and every day, find meaning and joy in large and small things
- Today and every day, enjoy and show appreciation for your friends, family, and fellow human beings
- Today and every day, follow your dreams and true purpose
- Limit your expectations about the behavior of others

PART SIX:

FINAL THOUGHTS

Through the span of this book, a series of recurring themes emerged that define what great looks like in personal and professional development. Without excessive introduction, here are a set of practices that will build your character, accelerate your growth, and establish you as an execution expert. Above all else, remember, the journey is the reward.

Build Your Character

- Always be ethical, honest, and sincere
- Vigorously build and protect your reputation and credibility
- Actively listen with an open mind
- Scream your passion and paint your masterpiece

Accelerate Your Growth

- Define your goals and commit to lifelong learning
- Double down on strengths
- Aim for mastery but accept that it can never be attained

Establish Yourself As An Execution Expert

- Take calculated risks
- Execute and iterate
- Look for and shine the spotlight on bright spots

Recommended Reading
and References

Chapter One: Leadership

Getty, J. Paul, <u>How to Be Rich</u>, New York: Jove Books, 1986.

Dave Logan, et al. <u>Tribal Leadership: Leveraging Natural Groups to Build a Thriving Organization</u>. Harper Business, 2008.

Kouzes, James M.; Posner, Barry Z.. <u>The Leadership Challenge</u>. Jossey-Bass, 2008.

Maxwell, John C. <u>The 21 Irrefutable Laws of Leadership: Follow Them and People Will Follow You</u>. Thomas Nelson, 2007.

Bossidy, Larry; Charan, Ram; Burck, Charles. <u>Execution: The Discipline of Getting Things Done</u>. Crown Business, 2002.

Chapter Two: Problem Solving

The Presidential Commission on the Space Shuttle Challenger Accident Report, June 6, 1986.

Judge, Timothy A., Cable, Daniel M., "The Effect of Physical Height on Workplace Success and Income: Preliminary Test of a Theoretical Model." Journal of Applied Psychology, Vol 89(3), Jun 2004, 428-441.

Rasiel, Ph.D, Ethan; Friga, Paul N.. <u>The McKinsey Mind: Understanding and Implementing the Problem-Solving Tools and Management Techniques of the</u>

World's Top Strategic Consulting Firm The McKinsey Mind: Understanding and Implementing the Problem-Solving Tools and Management Techniques of the World's Top Strategic Consulting Firm. McGraw-Hill, 2001.

Chapter Three: People Management

Belkin, Douglas. "Talent Scouts For Cirque du Soleil Walk a Tightrope." The Wall Street Journal, September 8, 2007.

Smart, Geoff; Street, Randy. Who: The A Method for Hiring. Ballantine Books, 2008.

Buckingham, Marcus; Coffman, Curt. First, Break All the Rules: What the World's Greatest Managers Do Differently. Simon & Schuster, 1999.

Chapter Four: Change Management

Heath, Chip; Heath, Dan. Switch: How to Change Things When Change Is Hard. Crown Books, 2010.

Tversky, Amos; Kahneman, Daniel. "The Framing of Decisions and the Psychology of Choice." Science, New Series, Vol. 211, No. 4481. (Jan. 30, 1981), pp. 453-458.

Kotter , John P.. Leading Change Leading Change. Harvard Business Press, 1996.

Chapter Seven: Corporate Culture

Tony Hsieh. Delivering Happiness: A Path to Profits, Passion, and Purpose. Business Plus, 2010.

Chapter Nine: Customer Satisfaction and Loyalty

Anderson, Eugene W.; Fornell, Claes; Rust, Roland T. "Customer Satisfaction, Productivity, and Profitability: Difference Between Goods and Services." Marketing Science, Vol. 16, No.2, 1997, 129-145.

Reichheld, Fred. <u>The Ultimate Question: Driving Good Profits and True Growth</u>. Harvard Business Press, 2006.

Timothy L. Keiningham, et al. <u>Loyalty Myths: Hyped Strategies That Will Put You Out of Businessand Proven Tactics That Really Work</u>. Wiley, 2005.

Chapter Ten: Selling to Executives

Thull , Jeff. <u>Mastering the Complex Sale: How to Compete and Win When the Stakes are High!</u>. Wiley, 2003.

Thull, Jeff. <u>The Prime Solution: Close the Value Gap, Increase Margins, and Win the Complex Sale</u>. Kaplan Business, 2005.

Chapter Eleven: Messaging Effectiveness

Heath, Chip; Heath, Dan. <u>Made To Stick: Why Some Ideas Survive and Others Die</u>. Random House, 2007.

Vitale , Joe. <u>Hypnotic Writing: How to Seduce and Persuade Customers with Only Your Words</u>. Wiley, 2006.

Farhat-McHayleh, Nada et al. "Techniques for Managing Behaviour in Pediatric Dentistry: Comparative Study of Live Modeling and Tell–Show–Do Based on Children's Heart Rates during Treatment." Journal of the Canadian Dental Association, Vol. 75, No. 4, May 2009, 283-283f.

Chapter Thirteen: Webinars

Molay, Ken. "Best Practices for Webinars." Adobe whitepaper, 2009.

Chapter Fourteen: Building Digital Communities

Carter, Sandy. The New Language of Marketing 2.0: How to Use ANGELS to Energize Your Market. IBM Press, 2008.

Chapter Fifteen: Sales Force Effectiveness

DeVincentis, John. Rethinking the Sales Force: Redefining Selling to Create and Capture Customer Value. McGraw-Hill, 1999.

Chapter Sixteen: Negotiation

Cotter , Michael J.; Henley, Jr, James A. "First-Offer Disadvantage in Zero-Sum Game Negotiation Outcomes." Journal of Business-to-Business Marketing, Vol. 15(1) 2008, 25-44.

Chapter Seventeen: Statistical Uncertainty

Quinn , Graham E.; Shin , Chai H.; Maguire, Maureen G.; Stone , Richard A. "Myopia and ambient lighting at night." Nature, Vol. 399, 13 MAY 1999, 113-114.

Zadnik, Karla et al. "Vision: Myopia and ambient night-time lighting." Nature Vol. 404, 9 March 2000, 143-144.

Ropeik, David. How Risky Is It, Really: Why Our Fears Don't Always Match the Facts. McGraw Hill, 2010.

Chapter Nineteen: Mergers and Acquisitions

Five Frogs on a Log : A CEO's Field Guide to Accelerating the Transition in Mergers, Acquisitions, and Gut Wrenching Change by: Mark L. Feldman, Michael F. Spratt, Michael Frederick Spratt

Cambridge Associates, LLC. "Private Equity and Venture Capital Funds Closed Out the First Half of 2010 with 5th Consecutive Quarter of Positive Returns." Press Release, 17 November 2010.

Chapter Twenty Two: Brainstorming

Osborn, Alex. Your Creative Power. Myers Press, 2007.

Osborn, Alex. Applied Imagination: Principles and Procedures of Creative Problem-Solving 3rd Edition. Creative Education Foundation, 1993.

Litchfield, Robert C.. "Brainstorming rules as assigned goals: Does brainstorming really improve idea quantity?" Motiv Emot (2009) 33:25–31.

Chapter Twenty Three: Entrepreneurship

Gerber , Michael E..The E-Myth Revisited: Why Most Small Businesses Don't Work and What to Do About It. HarperCollins, 1995.

Kawasaki , Guy. The Art of the Start: The Time-Tested, Battle-Hardened Guide for Anyone Starting Anything. Portfolio Hardcover, 2004.

Randy Komisar. The Monk and the Riddle: The Art of Creating a Life While Making a Living. Harvard Business Press, 2001.

Johnson, Steven. Where Good Ideas Come From: The Natural History of Innovation. Riverhead Hardcover, 2010.

Port, Michael. Book Yourself Solid. John Wiley & Sons, 2006.

Chapter Twenty Five: Public Speaking

Koegel, Timothy J.. <u>The Exceptional Presenter: A Proven Formula to Open Up and Own the Room</u>. Greenleaf Book Group Press, 2007.

Mavity, Roger; Bayley, Stephen. <u>Life's a Pitch: How to Sell Yourself and Your Brilliant Ideas</u>. Corgi, 2009.

Reynolds, Garr. <u>Presentation Zen Design: Simple Design Principles and Techniques to Enhance Your Presentations</u>. New Riders Press, 2009.

Duarte, Nancy. <u>slide:ology: The Art and Science of Creating Great Presentations</u>. O'Reilly Media, 2008.

Chapter Twenty Six: Storytelling

Simmons, Annette; Lipman, Doug. <u>The Story Factor</u>. Basic Books, 2006.

Chapter Twenty Seven: Body Language

Navarro, Joe; Karlins, Marvin. <u>What Every BODY is Saying: An Ex-FBI Agent's Guide to Speed-Reading People</u>. Harper Paperbacks, 2008.

Chapter Twenty Eight: Charisma

Carnegie, Dale. <u>How To Win Friends and Influence People</u>. Simon & Schuster, 2009.

Monarth, Harrison. <u>Executive Presence: The Art of Commanding Respect Like a CEO</u>

<u>Harrison Monarth</u>. McGraw-Hill, 1999.

McNally, David; Speak, Karl. <u>Be Your Own Brand</u>, Berrett-Koehler Publishers, 2003.

Cialdini, Robert. <u>Influence: Science and Practice</u>. Prentice Hall, 2008.

Levine, Michael; James, Lloyd, <u>Charming Your Way To The Top</u>. Lyons Press, 2004.

Hornik, Jacob; Ellis, Shmuel. "Strategies to Secure Compliance for a Mall Intercept Interview." Public Opinion Quarterly, Vol. 52, 1988, 539-551.

Chapter Twenty Nine: Happiness and Meaning

Frankl, Viktor E. <u>Man's Search for Meaning</u>. Boston: Beacon Press, 2006.

Made in the USA
Charleston, SC
27 May 2011